Contenu

C000066821

High-frequency words ....

Module 1
Words I should know for speaking and writing activities **15**
Extra words I should know for reading and listening activities **18**

Module 2
Words I should know for speaking and writing activities **19**
Extra words I should know for reading and listening activities **22**

Module 3
Words I should know for speaking and writing activities **23**
Extra words I should know for reading and listening activities **26**

Module 4
Words I should know for speaking and writing activities **27**
Extra words I should know for reading and listening activities **30**

Module 5
Words I should know for speaking and writing activities **31**
Extra words I should know for reading and listening activities **34**

Module 6
Words I should know for speaking and writing activities **35**
Extra words I should know for reading and listening activities **38**

Module 7
Words I should know for speaking and writing activities **39**
Extra words I should know for reading and listening activities **42**

Module 8
Words I should know for speaking and writing activities **43**
Extra words I should know for reading and listening activities **46**

High-frequency words

Common –er verbs

accepter	to accept
adorer	to love, to adore
aider	to help
aimer	to like
aller	to go
aller à pied	to walk
allumer	to light, to turn, to switch on
améliorer	to improve
(s)'arrêter	to stop

Had a look ☐ **Nearly there** ☐ **Nailed it** ☐

chanter	to sing
chercher	to look for
cliquer	to click (ICT)
coller	to stick
commander	to order
compter/compter sur	to count, to intend, to count on (someone)
contacter	to contact
continuer	to continue, to carry on
copier	to copy
se coucher	to go to bed
coûter	to cost

Had a look ☐ **Nearly there** ☐ **Nailed it** ☐

se débrouiller	to cope, to manage, to get by
décider	to decide
décoller	to take off (plane)
se dépêcher	to hurry
dépenser	to spend (money)
se déshabiller	to get undressed
désirer	to want, to desire
dessiner	to draw
détester	to hate
discuter	to discuss
donner	to give
durer	to last

Had a look ☐ **Nearly there** ☐ **Nailed it** ☐

s'échapper	to escape
écouter	to listen
écraser	to squash
empêcher	to prevent
endommager	to harm, to damage
entrer	to enter, to go in
envoyer	to send
espérer	to hope

essayer	to try
étudier	to study
expliquer	to explain

Had a look ☐ **Nearly there** ☐ **Nailed it** ☐

se fâcher	to get angry
fermer	to close, to switch off
frapper	to knock, to hit
gagner	to earn, to win
garder	to look after, to mind (child, dog)
garer	to park
gérer	to manage (business)
s'habiller	to get dressed
habiter	to live (inhabit)
informer	to inform
inviter	to invite
jeter	to throw

Had a look ☐ **Nearly there** ☐ **Nailed it** ☐

laisser	to leave behind (an object)
(se) laver	to wash
se lever	to get up
louer	to rent, to hire
manger	to eat
manquer	to miss, to be lacking
marcher	to walk, to work (function)
mériter	to deserve
monter	to climb, to get on(to), to go up
monter (dans)	to get into (bus, car, train)
montrer	to show
nettoyer	to clean
noter	to note

Had a look ☐ **Nearly there** ☐ **Nailed it** ☐

s'occuper de	to look after
organiser	to organise
ôter	to take off (clothes etc.)
oublier	to forget, to leave something behind
pardonner	to forgive
parler	to speak
passer	to pass, to spend (time)
penser	to think (about)
peser	to weigh
pleurer	to cry
porter	to wear
poser	to place
pousser	to push
préférer	to prefer

présenter	to introduce (a person), to present
prêter	to lend
se promener	to go for a walk
quitter	to leave (somewhere, somebody)

Had a look ☐ **Nearly there** ☐ **Nailed it** ☐

raconter	to tell, to recount
se rappeler	to remember
rater	to fail, to miss (train, bus, etc.)
rechercher	to research
recommander	to recommend
regretter	to regret, to be sorry
rembourser	to refund
remercier	to thank
remplacer	to replace
rencontrer	to meet
rentrer (à la maison)	to return (home), to go back (home)
renverser	to knock over
réparer	to repair
répéter	to repeat
se reposer	to rest
réserver	to reserve
ressembler	to look like, to resemble
rester	to stay
retourner (à l'école)	to return (to school), to go back (to school)
se réveiller	to wake up
rouler	to go (in a car)

Had a look ☐ **Nearly there** ☐ **Nailed it** ☐

sauter	to jump
sauver	to save
sembler	to seem
signer	to sign
signifier	to mean, to signify
sonner	to ring (a bell)
souhaiter	to wish
stationner	to park
téléphoner	to phone
(se) terminer	to end
tirer	to pull
tomber	to fall
toucher	to touch
travailler	to work
traverser	to cross, to go across
trouver	to find
utiliser	to use
vérifier	to check

voler	to fly, to steal
voyager	to travel

Had a look ☐ **Nearly there** ☐ **Nailed it** ☐

Common –ir verbs

atterrir	to land
choisir	to choose
s'endormir	to fall asleep
finir	to finish, to end
nourrir	to feed, to nourish
offrir	to offer, to give a present/ gift
ouvrir	to open
partir	to leave, to depart
prévenir	to warn
remplir	to fill, to fill in
réussir	to succeed
se servir de	to use
sortir	to go out
se souvenir	to remember
tenir	to hold
venir	to come

Had a look ☐ **Nearly there** ☐ **Nailed it** ☐

Common –re verbs

apprendre	to learn
attendre	to wait for
boire	to drink
conduire	to drive
connaître	to know (person, place)
décrire	to describe
descendre (de)	to get out of (bus, car, train)
dire	to tell, to say
entendre	to hear
éteindre	to switch off
(se) faire mal	to hurt (oneself)
introduire	to introduce (an item, an idea)
lire	to read

Had a look ☐ **Nearly there** ☐ **Nailed it** ☐

mettre	to put
plaire (à)	to please
prendre	to take
produire	to produce
remettre	to put back
répondre	to reply
rire	to laugh
sourire	to smile

5

suivre	to follow
vivre	to live
vendre	to sell

Had a look ☐ **Nearly there** ☐ **Nailed it** ☐

Common –oir verbs

avoir	to have
avoir besoin de	to need
avoir l'intention de (faire)	to mean to (do)
devoir	to have to, must
savoir	to know (a fact)
voir	to see
vouloir	to want

Had a look ☐ **Nearly there** ☐ **Nailed it** ☐

Common adjectives: describing someone

actif/-ve	active
agréable	pleasant
amical(e)	friendly
bavard(e)	talkative
bête	silly
calme	peaceful, quiet, calm
désagréable	unpleasant
drôle	funny (comical)
égoïste	selfish
généreux/-euse	generous
gentil(le)	kind
gros(se)	fat
honnête	honest
indépendant(e)	independent
intelligent(e)	intelligent, clever
joli(e)	pretty
laid(e)	ugly
marrant(e)	funny (comical)
méchant(e)	naughty
mince	slim

Had a look ☐ **Nearly there** ☐ **Nailed it** ☐

moche	ugly
mûr(e)	mature
optimiste	optimistic
paresseux/-euse	lazy
(im)patient(e)	(im)patient
pessimiste	pessimistic
petit(e)	small, short (person)
(im)poli(e)	(im)polite
populaire	popular
responsable	responsible
rigolo(te)	funny (comical)
sage	good (well-behaved), wise

sérieux/-euse	serious
sévère	strict
strict(e)	strict
sympa (invariable)	nice, likeable
sympathique	nice, likeable
timide	shy
travailleur/-euse	hard-working
vilain(e)	naughty

Had a look ☐ **Nearly there** ☐ **Nailed it** ☐

Common adjectives: I am, you are, we are …

célèbre	famous
content(e)	pleased
de bonne humeur	in a good mood
étonné(e)	surprised
faible (en maths, etc.)	weak (in maths, etc.)
fatigué(e)	tired
fort(e) (en maths, etc.)	strong (in maths, etc.)
heureux/-euse	happy, content
inquiet/-iète	worried
jeune	young
malheureux/-euse	unhappy
perdu(e)	lost
pressé(e)	in a hurry
reconnaissant(e)	grateful
riche	rich
satisfait(e)	satisfied
sauf/-ve	safe
surpris(e)	surprised
triste	sad
vieux/vieil/vieille	old

Had a look ☐ **Nearly there** ☐ **Nailed it** ☐

Common adjectives: opinions

amusant(e)	fun, amusing
bruyant(e)	noisy
cher/-ère	expensive
chouette	great (fantastic)
démodé(e)	old fashioned
dur(e)	hard
effrayant(e)	frightening
facile	easy, simple
fantastique	fantastic
fatigant(e)	tiring
favori(te)	favourite
formidable	great (marvellous)
génial(e)	great (fantastic)
idéal(e)	ideal
incroyable	unbelievable

injuste	*unfair*
inutile	*useless*
juste	*fair*

Had a look ☐ **Nearly there** ☐ **Nailed it** ☐

magnifique	*magnificent*
malsain(e)	*unhealthy*
merveilleux/-euse	*marvellous*
nécessaire	*necessary*
négatif/-ve	*negative*
parfait(e)	*perfect*
passionnant(e)	*exciting*
positif/-ve	*positive*
pratique	*practical*
préféré(e)	*favourite*
raisonnable	*reasonable*
ridicule	*ridiculous*
sain(e)	*healthy (food/way of life)*
sensationnel(le)	*sensational*
sensass	*sensational*
simple	*easy, simple*
super	*great (fantastic)*
superbe	*superb*
utile	*useful*
valable	*valid*
vrai(e)	*true*

Had a look ☐ **Nearly there** ☐ **Nailed it** ☐

Other common adjectives

à la mode	*fashionable*
ancien(ne)	*former, old*
autre	*other*
chaud(e)	*hot*
court(e)	*short*
d'une grande valeur	*valuable*
dernier/-ière	*last*
étroit(e)	*thin, narrow*
fermé à clef	*locked*
grand(e)	*large, big*
gratuit(e)	*free (at no cost)*
grave	*serious*
gros(se)	*large, big*
haut(e)	*high, tall (building)*
léger/-ère	*light*
libre	*free (unoccupied, available)*
long(ue)	*long*
lourd(e)	*heavy*

Had a look ☐ **Nearly there** ☐ **Nailed it** ☐

même	*same*
moderne	*modern*

mouillé(e)	*wet*
mûr(e)	*ripe*
neuf/-ve	*new (brand new)*
nombreux/-euse	*numerous*
normal(e)	*normal*
nouveau/nouvel/nouvelle	*new*
ouvert(e)	*open*

Had a look ☐ **Nearly there** ☐ **Nailed it** ☐

pareil(le)	*alike, the same*
plein(e)	*full*
pourri(e)	*rotten*
prêt(e)	*ready*
prochain(e)	*next*
propre	*own*
rangé(e)	*tidy*
rapide	*fast*
récent(e)	*recent*
reconnu(e)	*recognised, well known*
réel(le)	*real*
silencieux/-ieuse	*silent*
situé(e)	*situated*
tranquille	*peaceful, quiet, calm*
type	*typical*

Had a look ☐ **Nearly there** ☐ **Nailed it** ☐

Comparisons/Superlatives

plus/moins	*more/less*
plus que/moins que	*more than/less than*
bon/meilleur/le meilleur	*good/better/best*
mauvais/pire/le pire	*bad/worse/worst*
bien/mieux/le mieux	*well/better/best*
mal/plus mal/le plus mal	*badly/worse/worst*
beaucoup/plus/le plus	*a lot, lots/more/the most*
peu/moins/le moins	*few, little/less/the least*

Had a look ☐ **Nearly there** ☐ **Nailed it** ☐

Common adverbs

à peine	*hardly*
assez	*fairly, quite*
aussi	*too, as well*
trop	*too*
bien	*well*
bientôt	*soon*
bon marché	*cheap(ly)*
d'habitude	*usually*
debout	*standing*
déjà	*already*
encore	*again*
ensemble	*together*

fort	*loud(ly)*	contre	*against*
(mal)heureusement	*(un)fortunately*	dans	*in (inside)*
ici	*here*	de	*from*
immédiatement	*immediately*	dehors	*outside*
jamais	*never*		
là	*there*		

Had a look ☐   **Nearly there** ☐   **Nailed it** ☐

là-bas	*over there*	depuis	*since, for*
là-haut	*up there*	derrière	*behind*
longtemps	*(for) a long time*	devant	*in front of, in the front*

Had a look ☐   **Nearly there** ☐   **Nailed it** ☐

normalement	*usually*	en	*in, within (time)*
nulle part	*nowhere*	en dehors de	*outside (of)*
partout	*everywhere*	en face de	*opposite*
pas encore	*not yet*	en haut	*above*
peut-être	*perhaps*	en-dessous	*under/underneath*
plutôt	*rather*	entre	*between*
presque	*almost*	jusqu'à	*until*
quelque part	*somewhere*	loin de	*far from*
quelquefois	*sometimes*	malgré	*despite, in spite of*
rarement	*rarely*	nulle part	*nowhere*
récemment	*recently*	par	*through*
souvent	*often*	parmi	*among(st)*
surtout	*especially*	pour	*for, in order to*
toujours	*always, still*	près (de)	*near (to)*
tout de suite	*straight away, immediately*	sans	*without*
très	*very*	selon	*according to*
vite	*quickly*	sous	*under/underneath*
vraiment	*really*	sur	*on (on top of)*
		vers	*towards*

Had a look ☐   **Nearly there** ☐   **Nailed it** ☐

Had a look ☐   **Nearly there** ☐   **Nailed it** ☐

Prepositions

Connectives

à	*at, to*	à cause de	*because of*
à côté de	*next to*	à part	*apart from*
à partir de	*from*	ainsi	*so, therefore*
à travers	*across*	alors	*so, therefore, then*
après	*after*	aussi	*also*
au bord de	*at the side/edge of*	car	*because*
au bout de	*at the end of*	cependant	*however*
au fond	*in the background, at the back*	c'est-à-dire	*that is to say, i.e.*
au fond de	*at the back of, at the bottom of*	comme	*as, like*
		d'un côté/de l'autre côté	*on the one hand/on the other hand*
au lieu de	*instead of*	donc	*so, therefore*
au milieu (de)	*in the middle (of)*		

Had a look ☐   **Nearly there** ☐   **Nailed it** ☐

au premier plan	*in the foreground*	ensuite	*next*
au-dessus de	*above*	évidemment	*obviously*
autour de	*around*	mais	*but*
avant	*before*	même si	*even if*
avec	*with*	ou	*or*
chez	*at (someone's house)*	par contre	*on the other hand*

par exemple	for example
pendant que	while
pourtant	however
puis	then
puisque	seeing that, since
quand	when
sans doute	undoubtedly, without doubt, probably
si	if
y compris	including

Had a look ☐ **Nearly there** ☐ **Nailed it** ☐

Numbers

un(e)	1
deux	2
trois	3
quatre	4
cinq	5
six	6
sept	7
huit	8
neuf	9
dix	10
onze	11
douze	12
treize	13
quatorze	14
quinze	15
seize	16
dix-sept	17
dix-huit	18
dix-neuf	19

Had a look ☐ **Nearly there** ☐ **Nailed it** ☐

vingt	20
vingt et un	21
vingt-deux	22
vingt-trois	23
vingt-quatre	24
vingt-cinq	25
vingt-six	26
vingt-sept	27
vingt-huit	28
vingt-neuf	29
trente	30
trente et un	31
trente-deux, etc.	32, etc.
quarante	40
cinquante	50
soixante	60

Had a look ☐ **Nearly there** ☐ **Nailed it** ☐

soixante-dix	70
soixante et onze	71
soixante-douze	72
soixante-treize	73
soixante-quatorze	74
soixante-quinze	75
soixante-seize	76
soixante-dix-sept	77
soixante-dix-huit	78
soixante-dix-neuf	79

Had a look ☐ **Nearly there** ☐ **Nailed it** ☐

quatre-vingts	80
quatre-vingt-un	81
quatre-vingt-deux, etc.	82, etc.
quatre-vingt-dix	90
quatre-vingt-onze	91
quatre-vingt-douze, etc.	92, etc.

Had a look ☐ **Nearly there** ☐ **Nailed it** ☐

cent (m)	100
cent un(e)	101
cent vingt	120
deux cents	200
mille (m)	1000
mille cent	1100
deux mille	2000
un million (m)	1,000,000
deux millions (m)	2,000,000
premier/-ière	first
deuxième	second
onzième	eleventh
vingt-et-unième	twenty -first

Had a look ☐ **Nearly there** ☐ **Nailed it** ☐

Opinions

à mon avis	in my opinion
absolument	absolutely
bien entendu	of course
bien sûr	of course
ça dépend	that depends
ça m'énerve	it gets on my nerves
ça me fait rire	it makes me laugh
ça me plaît	I like it
ça m'est égal	it's all the same to me
ça ne me dit rien	it means nothing to me, I don't fancy that, I don't feel like it
ça suffit	that's enough
ça ne fait rien	it doesn't matter
ce n'est pas la peine	it's not worth it

d'accord	OK (in agreement)	quelqu'un	someone
j'en ai assez/marre	I've had enough	quelque chose	something
personnellement	personally	sauf	except
		la sorte	type (kind of)
		tout le monde	everybody

Had a look ☐ **Nearly there** ☐ **Nailed it** ☐

Had a look ☐ **Nearly there** ☐ **Nailed it** ☐

Other useful expressions

à bientôt	see you soon
à demain/vendredi	see you tomorrow/on Friday
bonne chance	good luck
bon courage	good luck
Ça s'écrit comment?	How do you spell that?
ça va	I'm fine, it's OK
comme çi, comme ça	so-so
désolé(e)	sorry
défense de	you are not allowed to
dommage	what a shame
excuse-/excusez-moi	(I'm) sorry (informal/formal)
il est interdit de	you are not allowed to

Had a look ☐ **Nearly there** ☐ **Nailed it** ☐

il faut	you must/one must
il y a	there is/are
je ne comprends pas	I don't understand
je ne sais pas	I don't know
merci (bien)	thank you (very much)
Qu'est-ce que cela veut dire?	What does that mean?
avec plaisir	with pleasure
tant mieux	all/so much the better
tant pis	too bad
voici	here is/are
voilà	there is/are (i.e. over there)
volontiers	with pleasure

Had a look ☐ **Nearly there** ☐ **Nailed it** ☐

Other useful little words

ça/cela	that
le chiffre	figure (number)
la chose	thing
comme	as, like
la façon	way (manner)
la fois	time (occasion)
le genre	type (kind of)
madame	Mrs, Madam
mademoiselle	Miss
monsieur	Mr, Sir
le nombre	number
le numéro	number (phone number)
par exemple	for example

Time, frequency and sequencing expressions

à … heure(s)	at … o'clock
à … heure(s) et quart	at quarter past …
à … heure(s) et demie	at half past …
à … heure(s) moins le quart	at quarter to …
à la fois	at the same time
à l'avenir	in future, from now on
à l'heure	on time
à temps partiel	part-time
l'an (m)	year
l'année (f)	year
après	after
après-demain	the day after tomorrow
après-midi	afternoon
aujourd'hui	today
auparavant	formerly, in the past
avant	before
avant-hier	the day before yesterday
bientôt	soon

Had a look ☐ **Nearly there** ☐ **Nailed it** ☐

d'abord	at first, firstly
dans le futur	in the future
d'habitude	usually
de bonne heure	early
le début	start
demain	tomorrow
dernier/-ière	last
de temps en temps	from time to time
déjà	already
de nouveau	again
en attendant	whilst waiting (for), meanwhile
en avance	in advance
en ce moment	at the moment
en retard	late
en train de (faire…)	(to be) doing
en même temps	at the same time
encore une fois	once more, again
enfin	at last, finally
environ	about, approximately

Had a look ☐ **Nearly there** ☐ **Nailed it** ☐

la fin	end
hier	yesterday
il y a	ago
le jour	day
la journée	day
le lendemain	the next day
longtemps	for a long time
maintenant	now
le matin	morning
le mois	month
normalement	normally
la nuit	night
parfois	sometimes
le passé	past
pendant	during
plus tard	later
presque	almost, nearly
prochain	next

Had a look ☐ **Nearly there** ☐ **Nailed it** ☐

quelquefois	sometimes
rarement	rarely
récemment	recently
la semaine	week
seulement	only
le siècle	century
le soir	evening
soudain	suddenly
souvent	often
suivant	following
sur le point de (être)	(to be) about to
tard	late
tôt	early
toujours	always, still
tous les jours	every day
tout à coup	suddenly, all of a sudden
tout de suite	immediately
vite	quickly

Had a look ☐ **Nearly there** ☐ **Nailed it** ☐

Question words

Comment?	How?
Combien (de)?	How much, How many?
Que?	What?
Qu'est-ce qui?	What? (as subject)
Qu'est-ce que?	What? (as object)
Quoi?	What?
De quelle couleur?	What colour?
Comment?	What like?
À quelle heure?	(At) what time?

Quel/Quelle?	What/Which?
Quand?	When?
Où?	Where?
Lequel/Laquelle/Lesquels/Lesquelles?	Which one(s)?
Qui?	Who?
Pourquoi?	Why?

Had a look ☐ **Nearly there** ☐ **Nailed it** ☐

Colours

blanc(he)	white
bleu(e)	blue
brun(e)	brown
châtain (invariable)	chestnut brown
clair(e)	light
foncé(e)	dark
gris(e)	grey
jaune	yellow
marron (invariable)	brown, chestnut brown
noir(e)	black
rose	pink
rouge	red
vert(e)	green
violet(te)	violet

Had a look ☐ **Nearly there** ☐ **Nailed it** ☐

Days, months and seasons of the year

lundi	Monday
mardi	Tuesday
mercredi	Wednesday
jeudi	Thursday
vendredi	Friday
samedi	Saturday
dimanche	Sunday

Had a look ☐ **Nearly there** ☐ **Nailed it** ☐

le mois	month
janvier	January
février	February
mars	March
avril	April
mai	May
juin	June
juillet	July
août	August
septembre	September
octobre	October
novembre	November
décembre	December

Had a look ☐ **Nearly there** ☐ **Nailed it** ☐

la saison	season
(au) printemps (m)	(in) spring
(en) été (m)	(in) summer
(en) automne (m)	(in) autumn
(en) hiver (m)	(in) winter

Had a look ☐ **Nearly there** ☐ **Nailed it** ☐

Quantities and measures

assez (de)	enough
beaucoup (de)	a lot (of), many
un centilitre	centilitre
un centimètre	centimetre
demi	half
une gramme	gramme
un kilomètre	kilometre
un mètre	metre
moins (de)	less
encore (de)	(some) more
pas mal (de)	quite a few
(un) peu (de)	a little of, few
plus (de)	more
plusieurs	several
le poids	weight
la quantité	quantity
un quart	quarter
quelques	some
un tiers	third
trop (de)	too much, too many

Had a look ☐ **Nearly there** ☐ **Nailed it** ☐

un kilo (de)	a kilo (of)
un litre (de)	a litre (of)
un morceau (de)	a piece (of)
un paquet (de)	a packet (of)
un peu (de)	a little (of)
un pot (de)	a jar (of)
une boîte (de)	a tin (of), a box (of)
une bouteille (de)	a bottle (of)
une centaine (de)	about a hundred
une douzaine (de)	a dozen
une tranche (de)	a slice (of)
une vingtaine (de)	about twenty

Had a look ☐ **Nearly there** ☐ **Nailed it** ☐

Countries

l'Algérie (f)	Algeria
l'Allemagne (f)	Germany
l'Angleterre (f)	England
l'Autriche (f)	Austria
la Belgique	Belgium

le Canada	Canada
la Chine	China
le Danemark	Denmark
la France	France
la Grande-Bretagne	Great Britain
la Grèce	Greece
la Hollande	Holland

Had a look ☐ **Nearly there** ☐ **Nailed it** ☐

l'Inde (f)	India
l'Irlande (f)	Ireland
l'Italie (f)	Italy
les Pays-Bas (m)	Netherlands
le Pakistan	Pakistan
la Russie	Russia
l'Écosse (f)	Scotland
le Sénégal	Senegal
l'Espagne (f)	Spain
la Suisse	Switzerland
la Tunisie	Tunisia
la Turquie	Turkey
le Royaume-Uni	United Kingdom
les États-Unis (m)	United States
le pays de Galles	Wales

Had a look ☐ **Nearly there** ☐ **Nailed it** ☐

Continents

l'Afrique (f)	Africa
l'Asie (f)	Asia
l'Australie (f)	Australia
l'Europe (f)	Europe
l'Amérique du Nord (f)	North America
l'Amérique du Sud (f)	South America

Had a look ☐ **Nearly there** ☐ **Nailed it** ☐

Nationalities

algérien(ne)	Algerian
allemand(e)	German
américain(e)	American
anglais(e)	English
autrichien(ne)	Austrian
belge	Belgian
britannique	British
canadien(ne)	Canadian
chinois(e)	Chinese
corse	Corsican
danois(e)	Danish
écossais(e)	Scottish
espagnol(e)	Spanish
européen(ne)	European

français(e)	French
gallois(e)	Welsh
grec(que)	Greek
hollandais(e)	Dutch

Had a look ☐   **Nearly there** ☐   **Nailed it** ☐

indien(ne)	Indian
irlandais(e)	Irish
italien(ne)	Italian
pakistanais(e)	Pakistani
russe	Russian
suisse	Swiss
tunisien(ne)	Tunisian
turque	Turkish

Had a look ☐   **Nearly there** ☐   **Nailed it** ☐

Geographical surroundings

à droite	on/to the right
à gauche	on/to the left
chez	at the house of
de chaque côté	from each side
de l'autre côté	from the other side
en bas	down(stairs)
en haut	up(stairs)
ici	here
là	there
là-bas	over there
la banlieue	suburb
la campagne	countryside
le centre-ville	town centre
la ville	town

Had a look ☐   **Nearly there** ☐   **Nailed it** ☐

loin de	far from
nulle part	nowhere
par	by
partout	everywhere
quelque part	somewhere
situé(e)	situated
tout droit	straight ahead
tout près	very near
toutes directions	all directions
l'est (m)	east
l'ouest (m)	west
le nord	north
le sud	south

Had a look ☐   **Nearly there** ☐   **Nailed it** ☐

Materials

l'argent (m)	silver
le béton	concrete

le bois	wood
le cuir	leather
le fer	iron
la laine	wool
l'or (m)	gold
la soie	silk
le verre	glass

Had a look ☐   **Nearly there** ☐   **Nailed it** ☐

Climate

l'averse (f)	shower
briller	to shine
le brouillard	fog
la brume	mist
la chaleur	heat
le ciel	sky
le climat	climate
couvert	overcast
doux	mild
l'éclair (m)	lightning
l'éclaircie (f)	bright spell
ensoleillé	sunny
faire beau	to be fine (weather)
faire mauvais	to be bad (weather)
geler	to freeze
la glace	ice
humide	humid, wet
la météo	weather forecast
mouillé	wet

Had a look ☐   **Nearly there** ☐   **Nailed it** ☐

neiger	to snow
le nuage	cloud
nuageux	cloudy
l'ombre (f)	shade, shadow
l'orage (m)	storm
orageux	stormy
pleuvoir	to rain
la pluie	rain
sec	dry
la tempête	storm
le temps	weather
le tonnerre	thunder
tremper	to soak
le vent	wind

Had a look ☐   **Nearly there** ☐   **Nailed it** ☐

Social conventions

à plus tard	see you later
à tout à l'heure	see you later

allô	*hello (on the telephone)*
amitiés	*best wishes*
amuse-toi/amusez-vous bien!	*enjoy yourself/yourselves!*
au revoir	*goodbye*
au secours!	*help!*
bien sûr	*of course*
bon voyage	*have a good journey*
bonjour	*hello, good morning*
bonne journée	*have a good day*
bonne nuit	*goodnight*
bonne soirée	*have a good evening*
bonsoir	*good evening*
de rien	*don't mention it*
Je t'/vous en prie	*It's a pleasure*
non merci	*no thank you*
pardon?	*I beg your pardon?, Pardon?*
prière de	*please (request – formal)*
le rendez-vous	*meeting, meeting place*
rendez-vous à six heures	*meet you at 6 o'clock*
s'il te plaît/s'il vous plaît	*please (informal)/please (polite)*
salut	*hi*
veuillez	*please (request – formal)*

Had a look ☐   **Nearly there** ☐   **Nailed it** ☐

Words I should know for speaking and writing activities

La famille	Family members
le beau-père	stepfather/father-in-law
la belle-mère	stepmother/mother-in-law
le beau-frère	brother-in-law
la belle-sœur	sister-in-law
le demi-frère	half-brother/stepbrother
la demi-sœur	half-sister/stepsister
la fille	daughter
le fils	son
l'enfant	child
le petit-enfant	grandchild
le mari	husband
l'ex mari (m)	ex-husband
la femme	wife
l'ex femme (f)	ex-wife

Had a look ☐   **Nearly there** ☐   **Nailed it** ☐

Les adjectifs de personnalité	Personality adjectives
Il/Elle est …	He/She is …
agaçant(e)	annoying
aimable	likeable
amusant(e)	amusing, funny
arrogant(e)	arrogant
bavard(e)	talkative, chatty
charmant(e)	charming
drôle	funny
égoïste	selfish
fidèle	loyal
fort(e)	strong

Had a look ☐   **Nearly there** ☐   **Nailed it** ☐

généreux/-euse	generous
gentil(le)	kind
impatient(e)	impatient
jaloux/-ouse	jealous
méchant(e)	nasty
paresseux/-euse	lazy
poli(e)	polite
sage	well-behaved, wise
sensible	sensitive
sérieux/-euse	serious
sympa (invariable)	nice
sympathique	nice
têtu(e)	stubborn, pig-headed
travailleur/-euse	hard-working
triste	sad

Had a look ☐   **Nearly there** ☐   **Nailed it** ☐

Ma description physique	My physical description
J'ai les cheveux …	I have … hair
courts/longs/mi-longs	short/long/mid-length
raides/bouclés/frisés	straight/curly
noirs/bruns/châtain	black/brown/chestnut
blonds/roux/gris/blancs	blond/red/grey/white
J'ai les yeux …	I have … eyes
bleus/verts	blue/green
gris/marron	grey/brown
J'ai …	I have …
des boutons	spots
une barbe	a beard
une moustache	a moustache
Je suis …	I am …
petit(e)/grand(e)	short/tall
de taille moyenne	of average height
mince/gros(se)	slim/fat
beau/belle	beautiful
joli(e)	pretty
moche	ugly
Je porte des lunettes	I wear glasses

Had a look ☐   **Nearly there** ☐   **Nailed it** ☐

En ville	In town
la boîte de nuit	nightclub
le bowling	bowling alley
le café	café
le centre commercial	shopping centre
le cinéma	cinema
les magasins (m)	shops
la patinoire	ice rink
la piscine	swimming pool
la plage	beach
le théâtre	theatre
dans	in
derrière	behind
devant	in front of
entre	between
en face de	opposite
à côté de	next to
près de	near

Had a look ☐   **Nearly there** ☐   **Nailed it** ☐

Quand?	When?
aujourd'hui	today
demain	tomorrow
après-demain	the day after tomorrow

M 1

ce matin	*this morning*
cet après-midi	*this afternoon*
ce soir	*tonight*

Had a look ☐ **Nearly there** ☐ **Nailed it** ☐

L'amitié — *Friendship*

Un(e) bon(ne) ami(e) est …	*A good friend is …*
de bonne humeur	*in a good mood*
compréhensif/-ive	*understanding*
équilibré(e)	*balanced, level-headed*
honnête	*honest*
indépendant(e)	*independent*
modeste	*modest*
patient(e)	*patient*
sûr(e) de lui/elle	*self-confident*
Un(e) bon(ne) ami(e) n'est pas …	*A good friend is not …*
de mauvaise humeur	*in a bad mood*
déprimé(e)	*depressed*
pessimiste	*pessimistic*
prétentieux/-euse	*pretentious*
vaniteux/-euse	*conceited*
Il/Elle …	*He/She …*
croit en moi	*believes in me*
dit toujours la vérité	*always tells the truth*
me fait rire	*makes me laugh*
prend soin de moi	*takes care of me*
voit le bon côté des choses	*sees the positive side of things*

Had a look ☐ **Nearly there** ☐ **Nailed it** ☐

Les traits de personnalité — *Qualities*

le sens de l'humour	*a sense of humour*
la patience	*patience*
la générosité	*generosity*
la gentillesse	*kindness*
la fidélité	*loyalty*
la modestie	*modesty*
l'honnêteté (f)	*honesty*
l'optimisme (m)	*optimism*

Had a look ☐ **Nearly there** ☐ **Nailed it** ☐

On décrit un(e) ami(e) — *Describing a friend*

Il/Elle …	*He/She …*
mesure 1,68 mètre	*is 1m 68cm tall*
semble timide	*seems shy*
porte un appareil dentaire	*has a brace*

a l'air cool	*looks cool*
a les yeux qui inspirent confiance	*has eyes which inspire (sb's) confidence*
On a les mêmes centres d'intérêt.	*We have the same interests.*

Had a look ☐ **Nearly there** ☐ **Nailed it** ☐

Les rapports de famille — *Family relationships*

se confier à	*to confide in*
se disputer avec	*to argue with*
s'entendre bien avec	*to get on well with*
se fâcher contre	*to get angry with*
s'intéresser à	*to be interested in*
s'occuper de	*to look after*
s'aimer	*to love each other*
se chamailler	*to bicker with each other*
mort(e)/décédé(e)	*dead*
divorcé(e)(s)	*divorced*
séparé(e)(s)	*separated*

Had a look ☐ **Nearly there** ☐ **Nailed it** ☐

On décrit sa famille — *Describing family members*

adorable	*adorable*
débrouillard(e)	*resourceful*
dynamique	*lively*
énergique/plein(e) d'énergie	*energetic*
extraverti(e)	*outgoing*
fragile	*fragile*
instable	*unstable*
introverti(e)	*introverted*

Had a look ☐ **Nearly there** ☐ **Nailed it** ☐

On va sortir — *Going out*

Je vais/Tu vas/On va…	*I'm going/You're going/We're going…*
aller au match	*to go to the match*
faire les magasins	*to go shopping*
faire du patin à glace/ du patinage	*to go ice-skating*
manger au fast-food	*to eat in a fast-food restaurant*
aller au cinéma	*to go to the cinema*
faire du skate	*to go skateboarding*
voir un spectacle	*to see a show*
jouer à des jeux vidéo	*to play video games*
venir chez moi	*to come to my house*
Tu veux venir?	*Do you want to come?*
Tu peux venir?	*Can you come?*

On se retrouve quand?	When will we meet?
... où?	Where ...?
... à quelle heure?	At what time ...?
Tu y vas avec qui?	Who are you going there with?
... comment?	How ...?
D'accord.	OK.
À plus!/À plus tard!	See you later!

Had a look ☐ **Nearly there** ☐ **Nailed it** ☐

On décrit une sortie / Describing a night out

hier soir	last night
à 20 heures	at 8 p.m.
d'abord	first of all
après	afterwards
puis/ensuite	then
J'ai .../Il/Elle a .../Nous avons ...	I .../He/She .../We ...
visité le musée	visited the museum
vu un match/une exposition	saw a match/an exhibition
mangé dans un restaurant	ate in a restaurant
refusé de manger	refused to eat
bu un coca	drank a cola
dit «au revoir»	said 'good-bye'
embrassé	kissed

Had a look ☐ **Nearly there** ☐ **Nailed it** ☐

Je suis .../Il/Elle est .../Nous sommes ...	I .../He/She .../We ...
allé(e)(s) à un pub	went to a pub
resté(e)(s) dehors sur la terrasse	stayed outside on the terrace
entré(e)(s) dans un restaurant	went into a restaurant
sorti(e)(s)	went out
parti(e)(s)	left
monté(e)(s) dans le bus	got on the bus
rentré(e)(s) à la maison	went home
tombé(e)(s) amoureux/-euse(s)	fell in love

Had a look ☐ **Nearly there** ☐ **Nailed it** ☐

Parler de son enfance / Talking about your childhood

Quand j'étais plus jeune, ...	When I was younger, ...
j'habitais avec (mon papa et ma maman)	I lived with (my mum and dad)
j'allais à l'école primaire	I went to primary school
j'avais (les cheveux blonds)	I had (blond hair)

j'étais (mignon(ne))	I was (cute)
je jouais (à «cache-cache»)	I played ('hide and seek')
j'aimais (les bonbons)	I liked (sweets)
je détestais (les épinards)	I hated (spinach)
je portais (un maillot du PSG)	I wore (a PSG shirt)
je rêvais d'être ...	my dream was to be a ...

Had a look ☐ **Nearly there** ☐ **Nailed it** ☐

Qui est-ce que tu admires? / Who do you admire?

Mon modèle s'appelle ...	My role model is called ...
Moi, j'admire ...	Personally I admire ...
Mon héros/Mon héroïne, c'est ...	My hero/heroine is ...
J'aimerais bien être comme lui/elle.	I would like to be like him/her.
J'admire sa créativité.	I admire his/her creativity.
Il/Elle ...	He/She ...
m'impressionne énormément	impresses me a lot
a travaillé très dur pour devenir ...	worked very hard to become ...
est devenu(e) ...	became ...
aide/a aidé ...	helps/helped ...
a/avait du courage/de la détermination	has/had courage/determination
est/était courageux/-euse face à des dangers terribles	is/was brave when faced with terrible danger
lutte/a lutté pour ...	fights/fought for ...
a obtenu ...	obtained/got ...
a sauvé la vie de ...	saved the life of ...
C'est un enfant adopté, comme moi.	He/She is adopted, like me.

Had a look ☐ **Nearly there** ☐ **Nailed it** ☐

17

Extra words I should know for reading and listening activities

Les descriptions — *Descriptions*

laid(e)*	*ugly*
têtu(e)	*stubborn*
instable	*unstable*
débrouillard(e)	*resourceful*
extraverti(e)	*extrovert*
introverti(e)	*introvert*
agaçant(e)	*annoying*
fidèle	*loyal*
honnête	*honest*
sage	*wise*
curieux/-euse	*curious*
déprimant(e)	*depressing*
défavorisé(e)	*underprivileged*
émouvant(e)	*touching*
fascinant(e)	*fascinating*
turbulent(e)	*boisterous*

Had a look ☐ **Nearly there** ☐ **Nailed it** ☐

Les expressions idiomatiques — *Idioms*

maigre comme un clou	*as thin as a rake*
le top du top!	*the best!*

Had a look ☐ **Nearly there** ☐ **Nailed it** ☐

Les noms — *Nouns*

le héros	*hero*
l'héroïne (f)	*heroine*
le modèle	*model, example*
la légende	*legend, caption*
les traits	*characteristics*
des reflets roux	*red highlights*
des sabots	*clogs*
la couture	*sewing*
le foulard	*(head)scarf*
à un très jeune âge	*at a very young age*

Had a look ☐ **Nearly there** ☐ **Nailed it** ☐

Les verbes — *Verbs*

admirer	*to admire*
prendre soin de	*to take care of*
se chamailler	*to argue*
porter	*to wear*
dire la vérité	*to tell the truth*
croire en quelqu'un	*to believe in someone*
briser en morceaux	*to break into pieces*
diffuser	*to broadcast*
envoyer	*to send*
libérer	*to free*
voir le bon côté	*to see the good side*
rêver de	*to dream of*
se fâcher contre	*to be angry with*
captiver	*to captivate*
tomber amoureux/ -euse de**	*to fall in love with*
se confier à quelqu'un**	*to confide in someone*
refuser de faire quelque chose**	*to refuse to do something*
trouver quelque chose ...	*to find/think something is ...*

Had a look ☐ **Nearly there** ☐ **Nailed it** ☐

⭐ *Many adjectives are cognates, i.e. words that are the same or similar in two languages but beware of false friends too!

The masculine adjective *laid* means 'ugly' and the last letter *d* is silent so watch out for the pronunciation.

⭐ **Remember that verbs in French don't always have the same prepositions after them that verbs in English do, for example:

to fall in love with *tomber amoureux de* ... (to fall in love of ...)

Words I should know for speaking and writing activities

**M
2**

Le sport — *Sport*

Le sport	Sport
Je fais …	I do/go …
du canoë-kayak	canoeing, kayaking
du footing	jogging
du hockey sur glace	ice hockey
du patinage	skating
du roller	roller skating
du vélo/cyclisme	cycling
de la boxe	boxing
de la danse	dancing
de la musculation	weightlifting
de la natation	swimming
de la planche à voile	windsurfing
de la voile	sailing
de l'escalade	climbing
de l'équitation	horse-riding
des randonnées	for walks
Je trouve ça …	I think it's …
bien/cool	good/cool
génial/super	great/super
passionnant	exciting
barbant/ennuyeux	boring
nul/stupide	rubbish/stupid

Had a look ☐ **Nearly there** ☐ **Nailed it** ☐

La musique — *Music*

La musique	Music
Je joue …	I play …
du piano	the piano
du saxophone	the saxophone
du violon	the violin
de la batterie	drums
de la clarinette	the clarinet
de la flûte	the flute
de la guitare	the guitar
de la trompette	the trumpet
de l'accordéon	the accordion
Mon chanteur préféré, c'est …	My favourite singer is …
car j'aime ses paroles/ ses mélodies	because I like his/her lyrics/tunes
J'aime aussi la musique de …	I also like … 's music.
Ça me donne envie de …	It makes me want to …
Ça me rend …	It makes me …
J'ai téléchargé/acheté …	I downloaded/bought …
Je n'aime pas du tout la musique de …	I don't like … 's music at all.
Je déteste …	I hate …

Had a look ☐ **Nearly there** ☐ **Nailed it** ☐

La technologie — *Technology*

La technologie	Technology
Je fais …	I do …
beaucoup de choses	lots of things
des quiz/des recherches pour mes devoirs	quizzes/research for my homework
Je fais des achats.	I buy things/make purchases.
Je vais sur mes sites préférés/des blogs/des forums.	I go on my favourite sites/ blogs/forums.
J'envoie des e-mails/ mails.	I send emails.
Je joue à des jeux en ligne.	I play games online.

Had a look ☐ **Nearly there** ☐ **Nailed it** ☐

Films et télé — *Films and TV*

Films et télé	Films and TV
J'aime/J'adore les …	I like/love …
Je (ne) suis (pas) fan de …	I am (not) a fan of …
Je n'aime pas …	I don't like …
J'ai une passion pour les …	I am passionate about …
J'ai horreur des …	I hate/can't stand …
films de gangsters/ d'action	gangster/action films
films d'aventure/ d'horreur	adventure/horror films
films d'arts martiaux	martial arts films
films de science-fiction	science fiction films
Je préfère …	I prefer …
les documentaires	documentaries
les jeux télévisés	game shows
les magazines	magazine programmes
les séries	series
les actualités	current affairs programmes
les émissions de musique/de sport/ jeunesse/de télé-réalité	music/sports/youth/ reality TV programmes
Mon émission préférée, c'est …	My favourite programme is …
Je trouve ça …	I find it …
Je pense que c'est …	I think that it's …

Had a look ☐ **Nearly there** ☐ **Nailed it** ☐

Parler de sport — *Talking about sport*

Parler de sport	Talking about sport
Je fais de l'escrime/du footing depuis (quatre ans).	I've been doing fencing/ jogging for (four years).
Je pratique le trampoline depuis (trois mois).	I've been trampolining for (three months).

19

M 2

On joue au basket ensemble depuis (trois ans).	We've been playing basketball together for (three years).
J'aime beaucoup ça car c'est ...	I like it a lot because it's ...
élégant/facile	elegant/easy
ludique/sympa	fun/nice
rapide/beau	fast/pleasant
C'est un sport qui est bon pour ...	It's a sport that is good for ...
le corps/le cœur	the body/the heart
le mental/la concentration	the mind/concentration
... et qui demande ...	... and which requires ...
une excellente forme physique	excellent physical condition
une bonne coordination	good coordination
de l'endurance	endurance
de bons réflexes	good reflexes
Ça m'aide à décompresser.	It helps me to relax.
Ça me fait du bien.	It does me good.
Je préfère les sports individuels.	I prefer individual sports.
Je respire.	I breathe.
Je me fixe des objectifs.	I set goals for myself.
J'oublie mes soucis.	I forget my worries.

Had a look ☐ **Nearly there** ☐ **Nailed it** ☐

Ma vie d'internaute

My life online

Je suis passionné(e) de ...	I am passionate about/a huge fan of ...
photographie/cinéma/musique	photography/cinema/music
Il y a (deux mois), j'ai créé ...	(Two months) ago, I created ...
une page Facebook	a Facebook page
une chaîne YouTube	a YouTube channel
une station de radio	a radio station
un blog	a blog
Ça (ne) marche (pas) très bien.	It's (not) working very well.
J'ai beaucoup d'abonnés et de mentions «J'aime».	I have lots of subscribers and likes.
Je vais travailler avec mon ami/ma sœur/prof ...	I'm going to work with my friend/sister/teacher ...
car il/elle est plus/moins ... que moi	because he/she is more/less ... than me
arrogant(e)/créatif/-ve	arrogant/creative
modeste/patient(e)	modest/patient
optimiste/organisé(e)	optimistic/organised
sérieux/-euse/technophobe	serious/technophobic
Nous allons créer ...	We're going to create ...

Had a look ☐ **Nearly there** ☐ **Nailed it** ☐

La lecture

Books and reading

Quand j'avais X ans, je lisais ...	When I was X years old, I read ...
J'aimais ...	I liked ...
Avant, avec mes enfants, on lisait ...	In the past, I read ... with my children.
des histoires/des romans	stories/novels
des livres illustrés/classiques	illustrated books/classics
des livres pour enfants/des journaux	children's books/newspapers
Maintenant, je lis ...	Now I read ...
sur ma tablette/mon ordi	on my tablet/my computer

Had a look ☐ **Nearly there** ☐ **Nailed it** ☐

Sur Internet

On the internet

Maintenant/Aujourd'hui, les jeunes ...	Now/Today, young people ...
lisent des blogs/des textos/des tweets	read blogs/texts/tweets
passent tout leur temps sur leur portable	spend all their time on their mobile
Je trouve ça génial.	I find that great.
Je trouve que c'est bien/mieux/un peu dommage.	I find that it's good/better/a bit of a shame.
À mon avis, Internet a tué les joies de la lecture.	In my opinion, the internet has killed the joy of reading.

Had a look ☐ **Nearly there** ☐ **Nailed it** ☐

Mes émissions préférées

My favourite TV programmes

Mon émission de télé préférée, c'est ...	My favourite TV programme is ...
C'est (un docu-réalité) qui parle de ...	It's (a reality documentary) about ...
Je le/la regarde ...	I watch it ...
toutes les semaines	every week
tous les jours/mois	every day/month
Je le/la trouve formidable/super/génial(e).	I find it amazing/fantastic/great.
Je ne le rate/manque jamais.	I never miss it.
Je ne le/la regarde jamais.	I never watch it.
Je le/la trouve débile/vulgaire.	I find it idiotic/crude.
J'adore les animateurs/animatrices.	I love the presenters.
Les acteurs sont excellents/ne sont pas crédibles.	The actors are excellent/not believable.
Le scénario n'a aucun rapport avec la réalité.	The script bears no relation to reality.

Je le/la regarde en version originale.	*I watch it in the original language.*
Avant, je regardais/nous regardions …	*Before, I/we used to watch …*
Maintenant, j'ai tendance à regarder …	*Now, I tend to watch …*
en direct sur la TNT	*live on terrestrial TV*
en replay/streaming	*recorded/streamed*

Had a look ☐   **Nearly there** ☐   **Nailed it** ☐

Le cinéma / *Cinema*

Je suis passionné(e) de cinéma.	*I'm passionate/mad about cinema.*
J'adore …	*I love …*
J'admire …	*I admire …*
Je suis fan de … depuis	*I'm a fan of … since*
Il est le plus …	*He is the most …*
Elle est la plus …	*She is the most …*
beau/belle	*good-looking, beautiful*
intelligent(e)	*intelligent*
talentueux/-euse	*talented*
élégant(e)	*elegant*
doué(e)	*gifted, talented*
célèbre	*famous*
chic	*chic*
Chez lui/elle, il y a très peu …	*With him/her, there is very little …*
de prétention	*pretentiousness*
de vanité	*vanity*
d'arrogance	*arrogance*

Had a look ☐   **Nearly there** ☐   **Nailed it** ☐

Il/Elle est extrêmement modeste/sincère/humble.	*He/she is extremely modest/sincere/humble.*
J'ai vu le film … il y a un moment et depuis, je suis fan.	*I saw the … film some time ago and since then, I've been a fan.*
Apparemment, quand il/elle était jeune …	*Apparently, when he/she was young …*
X compte parmi les acteurs les plus connus et les plus appréciés au monde.	*X is one of the best-known and best-regarded actors in the world.*
J'adore ses films et je les recommande.	*I love his/her films and I recommend them.*
Je vais voir son prochain film très bientôt.	*I'm going to see his/her next film very soon.*

Had a look ☐   **Nearly there** ☐   **Nailed it** ☐

M 2

Extra words I should know for reading and listening activities

Les descriptions	Descriptions
impatient(e)	impatient
charismatique	charismatic
arrogant(e)	arrogant
modeste	modest
créatif/-ve	creative
ludique	fun
motivant(e)	motivating
fédérateur/-rice	unifying
urbain(e)	urban
collectif/-ve	collective

Had a look ☐ **Nearly there** ☐ **Nailed it** ☐

Les nouvelles technologies	New technologies
les mentions (f)	likes
les abonné(e)s	subscribers
l'ambiance (f)	atmosphere
l'ordinateur/ordi (m)	computer
la chanson	song
le/la chanteur/-euse	singer
le portable	mobile phone
les blogs (m)*	blogs
les forums (m)*	forums
les réseaux sociaux (m)	social networks
les jeux en ligne (m)	online games
l'écran (m)	screen
la tablette*	tablet
la toile	the web
les textos (m)*	texts

Had a look ☐ **Nearly there** ☐ **Nailed it** ☐

Les idées	Concepts
la généalogie	genealogy
la souplesse	flexibility
le corps	body
le mental	mind
l'endurance (f)	endurance, stamina
la persévérance	perseverance
le projet	plan
les joies (f)	joys
la perte de temps	waste of time

Had a look ☐ **Nearly there** ☐ **Nailed it** ☐

Les expressions	Expressions
Ça m'énerve!**	That annoys me!
Ça m'amuse!**	That makes me laugh!
Ça marche bien!**	That works well!
Ça me passionne!**	That fascinates me!
Je décompresse!	I chill out!
Je suis passionné(e) de …	I'm a keen …
Je prends plaisir à …	I enjoy …

Had a look ☐ **Nearly there** ☐ **Nailed it** ☐

*Lots of new technology-related words are the same in French as in English, for example, *des blogs*.

**French people use *Ça* over and over in everyday language – try to learn as many expressions as you can with it in to increase your fluency!

Words I should know for speaking and writing activities

Repas et nourriture	Meals and food
Je bois/mange/prends …	I drink/eat/have …
du café/lait/jus d'orange	coffee/milk/orange juice
du pain grillé/beurre	toast/butter
du yaourt/miel	yogurt/honey
du poulet/jambon/poisson	chicken/ham/fish
du saucisson/fromage	sausage/cheese
du pain/riz	bread/rice
du chou-fleur/raisin	cauliflower/grapes
de la confiture/glace	jam/ice cream
de la soupe/viande	soup/meat
de la mousse au chocolat/tarte au citron	chocolate mousse/lemon tart
de l'eau (minérale) (f)	(mineral) water
des fruits (m)/bananes (f)	fruit/bananas
des fraises (f)/pêches (f)	strawberries/peaches
des pommes (f)/poires (f)	apples/pears
des légumes (m)/petits pois (m)	vegetables/peas
des champignons (m)/haricots verts (m)	mushrooms/green beans
des carottes (f)/pommes de terre (f)	carrots/potatoes
des céréales (f)/pâtes (f)	cereal/pasta
des crudités (f)/œufs (m)	crudités/eggs

Had a look ☐   **Nearly there** ☐   **Nailed it** ☐

Je ne mange pas de viande.	I don't eat meat.
Je suis végétarien(ne).	I'm vegetarian.
un paquet de …	a packet of …
un kilo de …	a kilo of …
une bouteille de …	a bottle of …
un pot de …	a jar/pot of …
cinq cents grammes de …	500 grams of …
quatre tranches de …	four slices of …
un morceau de …	a piece of …
un litre de …	a litre of …
une boîte de …	a tin/can of …
Il faut aller …	You need to go …
à la boucherie	to the butcher's
à la boulangerie	to the baker's
à la charcuterie	to the deli/pork butcher's
à la pâtisserie	to the cake shop
à l'épicerie (f)	to the grocer's
au marché	to the market

Had a look ☐   **Nearly there** ☐   **Nailed it** ☐

Les vêtements	Clothes
D'habitude, je porte …	Usually I wear …
Je vais mettre …	I'm going to put on …
J'ai mis …	I put on …
un blouson	a jacket
un chapeau	a hat
un collant	tights
un costume	a suit
un jean moulant	skinny jeans
un manteau	a coat
un pantalon	trousers
un polo	a polo shirt
un pull	a sweater

Had a look ☐   **Nearly there** ☐   **Nailed it** ☐

un sac à main	a handbag
un short	shorts
un sweat à capuche	a hoody
un tee-shirt	a T-shirt
une casquette	a cap
une ceinture	a belt
une chemise	a shirt
une cravate	a tie
une écharpe	a scarf
une mini-jupe	a mini-skirt
une robe	a dress
une veste	a jacket
des baskets (f)	trainers
des bottes (f)	boots
des chaussettes (f)	socks
des chaussures (f)	shoes
des gants (m)	gloves
des lunettes de soleil (f)	sunglasses

Had a look ☐   **Nearly there** ☐   **Nailed it** ☐

blanc(he)(s)	white
bleu(e)(s)	blue
gris(e)(s)	grey
jaune(s)	yellow
kaki	khaki
marron	brown
mauve(s)	purple
noir(e)(s)	black
orange	orange
rose(s)	pink
rouge(s)	red
vert(e)(s)	green
en coton/cuir/laine/soie	(made of) cotton/leather/wool/silk

M 3

M 3

rayé(e)	striped
à carreaux	checked
de marque	designer
habillé(e)	smart
de couleur vive	brightly-coloured
multicolore	multi-coloured
foncé(e)	dark

Had a look ☐ **Nearly there** ☐ **Nailed it** ☐

La vie quotidienne   *Daily life*

J'ai cours …	I have lessons …
tous les jours sauf …	every day except …
(cinq) jours par semaine	(five) days a week
Je vais au lycée …	I go to school …
en bus/en scooter/en voiture/à pied	by bus/by moped/by car/on foot
Les jours d'école, …	On school days …
je dois me lever tôt	I have to get up early
je prends mon petit-déjeuner	I have my breakfast
je quitte la maison	I leave the house
Le dimanche, …	On Sundays …
je peux rester au lit/faire la grasse matinée	I can stay in bed/have a lie-in
Le soir, …	In the evening …
je dois faire mes devoirs	I have to do my homework
je mange avec ma famille	I eat with my family
je regarde un peu la télé	I watch a bit of TV
Le mercredi/samedi après-midi, …	On Wednesday/Saturday afternoon …
je peux me détendre un peu	I can relax a bit
je reste à la maison/chez moi	I stay at home
Le week-end, …	At the weekend …
je sors avec mes copains	I go out with friends
je dois aider ma mère/mon père	I have to help my mum/dad
je vais au cinéma/au bowling	I go to the cinema/bowling

Had a look ☐ **Nearly there** ☐ **Nailed it** ☐

Les repas de fêtes   *Food for special occasions*

Ma fête préférée est …	My favourite festival is …
Noël/le 5 novembre/Hanoukka/Aïd el-Fitr/Diwali	Christmas/5 November/Hanukkah/Eid al-Fitr/Diwali
parce que j'adore …	because I love …
D'habitude, je le/la fête …	I usually celebrate it …

en famille/chez nous	with my family/at home
chez mon/ma/mes …/avec …	at my …'s house/with …
On fait/décore/se souhaite …	We do/decorate/wish each other …
D'abord, on mange/boit … suivi(e) par …	First we eat/drink …, followed by …
de la dinde	turkey
une bûche de Noël	Yule log
Dedans, il y a …	Inside, there is …
C'est mon/ma/mes … qui prépare(nt) …	My … prepare(s) …
Après le repas, on …	After the meal we …
s'offre (des cadeaux)	give each other (presents)
admire (le sapin de Noël)	admire the (Christmas tree)
chante/danse	sing/dance

Had a look ☐ **Nearly there** ☐ **Nailed it** ☐

Les repas à la maison   *Meals at home*

Du lundi au vendredi, je prends	From Monday to Friday I have
le petit-déjeuner à … heures.	breakfast at …
Le week-end, je prends mon petit-déjeuner plus tard.	At the weekend I have my breakfast later.
Je grignote après l'école.	I have a snack after school.
Je ne grignote jamais en dehors des repas.	I never snack between meals.
Je regarde la télé en mangeant le soir.	I watch TV while eating in the evening.
Dans ma famille, on ne regarde pas la télé en mangeant.	In our family, we don't watch TV while eating.
On dîne en famille tous les jours.	We have dinner as a family every day.

Had a look ☐ **Nearly there** ☐ **Nailed it** ☐

Félicitations!   *Congratulations!*

Je suis né(e) en …	I was born in …
Je viens de fêter …	I have just celebrated …
Il y a (trois) mois, j'ai fêté …	(Three) months ago I celebrated …
C'était mon quatorzième/quinzième anniversaire.	It was my fourteenth/fifteenth birthday.
J'ai reçu beaucoup de …	I received lots of …
J'ai invité … à un barbecue/une fête chez moi.	I invited … to a barbecue/party at my house.

Je suis allé(e) au mariage (de mon cousin) à la mairie avec toute ma famille. — *I went to (my cousin's) wedding at the town hall with all my family.*

On a mangé/écouté/dansé/joué/fait/vu ... — *We ate/listened to/danced/played/did/saw ...*

C'était une excellente soirée! — *It was an excellent evening!*

Pour fêter mon prochain anniversaire, je vais ... — *To celebrate my next birthday, I'm going to ...*

Had a look ☐   **Nearly there** ☐   **Nailed it** ☐

Les fêtes en France — *Festivals in France*

le jour férié — *public holiday*

le jour de l'An — *New Year's Day*

la fête des Rois/l'Épiphanie (f) — *Twelfth Night/Epiphany*

la Chandeleur — *Candlemas*

la Saint-Valentin — *St Valentine's Day*

Mardi Gras — *Shrove Tuesday*

1er Avril — *April Fool's Day*

Pâques — *Easter*

la fête du Travail — *May Day/Labour Day*

la fête des Mères — *Mother's Day*

la fête de la Musique — *music festival in France on 21 June*

la fête nationale — *Bastille Day, 14 July*

la Nuit Blanche — *first Saturday of October, when many museums and art galleries stay open all night*

la Toussaint — *All Saints' Day*

le jour de Noël — *Christmas Day*

la Saint-Sylvestre — *New Year's Eve*

Had a look ☐   **Nearly there** ☐   **Nailed it** ☐

M 3

Extra words I should know for reading and listening activities

La nourriture — *Food*

le chou-fleur	*cauliflower*
la bûche de Noël	*yule log*
le réveillon	*New Year's Eve meal*
la galette des rois	*special cake made to be eaten at Epiphany*
les verrines (f)	*verrines/tumblers/bite-size desserts*
la fève	*lucky charm put into the 'galette des rois'*
les épinards (m)	*spinach*
le saumon	*salmon*
la salade composée	*mixed salad*
le croquembouche	*profiterole-based dessert, built into a tower, quite often eaten as a cake at weddings*

Had a look ☐ **Nearly there** ☐ **Nailed it** ☐

Les jours de fête — *Celebrations*

la fête	*festivities, festival*
les noces d'argent (f)	*silver wedding anniversary*
la bague	*ring*
la mairie	*town hall*
le témoin	*witness*
le feu d'artifice	*fireworks*
le déguisement	*costume*
la reine	*queen*
les chars fleuris (m)	*flower-decked floats*
la Toussaint	*All Souls' Day (1 November)*
la Nuit Blanche	*an all-night or night-time arts festival, held every year in France on the first Saturday in October, where all museums, private and public art galleries and other cultural institutions are open free to the public*
le pays natal	*country of birth*

Had a look ☐ **Nearly there** ☐ **Nailed it** ☐

Décrire les fêtes — *Describing celebrations*

apprécié(e)	*appreciated*
partagé(e)	*shared*
attaché(e)	*attached*
élaboré(e)	*developed*
multicolore	*multicoloured*
prêt(e)	*ready*
loué(e)	*hired/rented*
gratuit(e)	*free*
alimentaire	*foodstuff*
pareil(le)	*same*
fier/-ière de	*proud of*
en soie*	*made of silk*
en laine*	*made of wool*
de marque*	*branded*
de couleur vive*	*brightly coloured*

Had a look ☐ **Nearly there** ☐ **Nailed it** ☐

Verbes — *Verbs*

se pacser	*to have a civil partnership*
grignoter	*to snack*
fêter	*to celebrate*
cacher	*to hide*
faire la grasse matinée	*to lie in*
être allergique à …	*to be allergic to …*
avoir horreur de …	*to hate …*
avoir lieu**	*to take place*
ajouter	*to add*
en mangeant …	*whilst eating …*

Had a look ☐ **Nearly there** ☐ **Nailed it** ☐

Les expressions idiomatiques — *Idioms*

Ne t'en fais pas!	*Don't worry about it!*
Et voilà!	*There you go!*

Had a look ☐ **Nearly there** ☐ **Nailed it** ☐

*Use *en* to refer to what something is made of.

Elle porte une robe en soie et lui un costume en laine.

Use the preposition *de* to indicate what type of item it is and to convey more description.

Benjamin aime les vêtements de marque et de couleur vive.

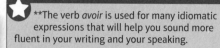

**The verb *avoir* is used for many idiomatic expressions that will help you sound more fluent in your writing and your speaking.

Examples: *avoir lieu* to take place; *en avoir marre* to have had enough.

La fête a lieu le 23 septembre. The festival takes place on the 23rd of September.

Le travail, c'est dur! J'en ai marre! Working is hard! I've had enough!

Words I should know for speaking and writing activities

Où j'habite
Where I live

J'habite ...	I live ...
Ma famille et moi habitons ...	My family and I live ...
On habite ...	We live ...
dans une ville historique/touristique	in an historic/touristy town
dans un petit village	in a small village
au bord de la mer	at the seaside
au centre-ville	in the town centre
à la campagne/montagne	in the countryside/mountains
en ville	in town
en Angleterre/Écosse/Irlande (du Nord)/Afrique	in England/Scotland/(Northern) Ireland/Africa
au Maroc/pays de Galles	in Morocco/Wales
aux Antilles	in the West Indies
à Paris/Birmingham	in Paris/Birmingham

Had a look ☐ **Nearly there** ☐ **Nailed it** ☐

dans le nord-est du/de la/de l'/des ...	in the north-east of ...
le nord/le nord-est	north/north-east
l'est/le sud-est	east/south-east
le sud/le sud-ouest	south/south-west
l'ouest/le nord-ouest	west/north-west
Dans ma région, il y a ...	In my region there is/are ...
des vignobles/stations de ski	vineyards/ski resorts
des collines/forêts	hills/forests
des fermes/champs	farms/fields
un port de pêche	a fishing port
un lac	a lake
C'est super parce qu'en hiver/en été, on peut (faire du ski/de l'escalade).	It's great because in winter/summer, you can (go skiing/climbing).

Had a look ☐ **Nearly there** ☐ **Nailed it** ☐

Le temps
Weather

Il fait beau/mauvais.	The weather's good/bad.
Il fait chaud/froid.	It's hot/cold.
Il y a du soleil.	It's sunny.
Il y a du brouillard/du vent.	It's foggy/windy.
Il y a un orage.	There's a storm.
Il pleut/neige/gèle.	It's raining/snowing/icy.
Ici, le climat est humide/sec.	Here, the climate is wet/dry.
Il peut faire très chaud/froid/doux.	It can be very hot/cold/mild.
Il ne fait pas trop chaud/froid ...	It's not too hot/cold ...

au printemps	in spring
en été/automne/hiver	in summer/autumn/winter

Had a look ☐ **Nearly there** ☐ **Nailed it** ☐

Les transports
Transport

Je vais/peux aller au collège ...	I go/can go to school ...
à pied/vélo	on foot/by bike
en train/métro/car/voiture/bus	by train/underground/coach/car/bus
Les transports en commun sont bons.	The public transport is good.

Had a look ☐ **Nearly there** ☐ **Nailed it** ☐

En ville
In town

Il y a ...	There is/are ...
un château	a castle
un centre de loisirs	a leisure centre
un marché	a market
un musée	a museum
un parc/jardin public	a (public) park
un stade	a stadium
un supermarché	a supermarket
un théâtre	a theatre
une bibliothèque	a library
une cathédrale	a cathedral
une église	a church
une gare (SNCF)	a (train) station
une mairie	a town hall
une mosquée	a mosque
une pharmacie	a chemist
une poste (un bureau de poste)	a post office
des hôtels	hotels

Had a look ☐ **Nearly there** ☐ **Nailed it** ☐

beaucoup de magasins	lots of shops
Il n'y a pas de ...	There isn't a/aren't any ...
Est-ce qu'il y a un/une/des ... près d'ici/par ici?	Is/Are there a/some ... near here?
Va/Allez tout droit.	Go straight on.
Tourne/Tournez à droite/gauche.	Turn right/left.
Prends/Prenez la première/deuxième droite/gauche.	Take the first/second road on the right/left.
Continue/Continuez jusqu'au carrefour/jusqu'aux feux	Continue as far as the crossroads/traffic lights
Traverse/Traversez la place/le pont.	Cross the square/bridge.
Descends/Descendez la rue.	Go down the road.
C'est ...	It's ...

M 4

(assez) loin/tout près — *(quite) a long way/very close*
sur ta/votre droite/ — *on your right/left*
gauche
au coin — *on the corner*
en face (du/de la/de l'/ — *opposite*
des)
à côté (du/de la/de l'/des) — *next to*

Had a look ☐ **Nearly there** ☐ **Nailed it** ☐

Ma région — *My region*

Ma région/Une région — *My region/A region that I*
que je connais bien, — *know well is …*
c'est …
C'est dans le (nord/sud) — *It's in the (north/south)*
de … — *of …*
près de la Manche/la — *near the English Channel/*
frontière allemande/ — *the German/Spanish*
espagnole — *border*
J'y habite depuis …/J'y — *I have lived there since*
vais … — *…/I have been going*
— *there …*
Le paysage/La côte est — *The landscape/coast*
vraiment magnifique/ — *is really wonderful/*
impressionnant(e). — *impressive.*
On peut y faire/visiter/ — *You can do/visit/see …*
voir … — *there.*
La région est connue — *The region is known for …*
pour …
Une personne célèbre — *A famous person who was*
qui est née en …, c'est … — *born in … is …*

Had a look ☐ **Nearly there** ☐ **Nailed it** ☐

Les renseignements — *Information*

Qu'est-ce qu'on va faire — *What are we going to do*
à …? — *in …?*
Je veux absolument — *I definitely want to (go on*
(faire une promenade — *a boat trip).*
en bateau).
J'ai envie de (louer un — *I feel like (hiring a boat).*
bateau).
Ça m'intéresse de — *I'm interested in seeing …*
voir …
Je tiens à (visiter — *I'm keen on (visiting the*
l'aquarium). — *aquarium).*
Je voudrais aller au/à — *I would like to go to …*
la/à l'/aux …
J'aimerais bien monter à — *I would like to go up …*
la/au …
Je ne veux pas rater/ — *I don't want to miss (the*
manquer (l'exposition — *exhibition on) …*
sur) …
Bonne idée. Pourquoi — *Good idea. Why not?*
pas?
Je veux bien faire ça — *I want to do that too.*
aussi.
D'accord. Ça m'est égal. — *OK. I don't mind.*

Ça ne me dit rien. — *I don't fancy that.*
Je n'en ai pas tellement — *I don't really feel like it.*
envie.
Ça a l'air nul! — *That sounds rubbish!*

Had a look ☐ **Nearly there** ☐ **Nailed it** ☐

Ville de rêve ou ville de cauchemar? — *Dream town or nightmare town?*

J'habite à … — *I live in …*
C'est un petit village/ — *It's a small village/big*
une grande ville dans … — *town in …*
J'habite dans la — *I live in the suburbs/a*
banlieue/un quartier — *district of …*
de …
Ce qui me plaît ici, c'est — *What I like is that …*
qu'il y a …
En été/hiver, on peut … — *In summer/winter, you*
— *can …*
Le problème, c'est que/ — *The problem is that …*
qu' …
il n'y a pas assez de — *there is/are not enough*
(magasins/espaces — *(shops/green spaces)*
verts)
il n'y a plus de (cinéma) — *there is/are no longer (a*
— *cinema)*
il n'y a ni (parc) ni (aire — *there is neither (a park)*
de jeux) — *nor (a play area)*
il n'y a aucun (bowling) — *there isn't a (single)*
— *(bowling alley)*
il n'y a aucune (zone — *there isn't a (single)*
piétonne) — *(pedestrian area)*
il n'y a qu'un seul — *there is only one (shop)*
(magasin)
il n'y a qu'une seule — *there is just one (street)*
(rue)
il n'y a rien pour les — *there is nothing for young*
jeunes — *people*
il n'y a pas grand-chose — *there's not a lot to do*
à faire

Had a look ☐ **Nearly there** ☐ **Nailed it** ☐

Il y a … — *There is/are …*
beaucoup de monde/de — *lots of people/cars*
voitures
trop de circulation/de — *too much traffic/too*
gens — *many people*
tellement de bruit/de — *so much noise/so many*
gens au chômage — *people out of work*
peu de travail/de — *not much work/public*
transports en commun/ — *transport/not many*
commerces — *businesses*
toujours des déchets — *always litter on the*
par terre — *ground*
plusieurs boîtes de nuit/ — *several nightclubs/cafés/*
cafés/restaurants — *restaurants*
Le bowling a fermé. — *The bowling alley has*
— *closed down.*

C'est sale/(trop) tranquille/très animé.
Ce n'est jamais tranquille.
Je trouve ça triste/déprimant/affreux/nul/désagréable.
En général, je (ne) suis (pas) content(e) de mon village/quartier/ma ville.

It's dirty/(too) quiet/very lively.
It's never quiet.
I find that sad/depressing/awful/rubbish/unpleasant.
In general, I am (not) happy with my village/district/town.

Had a look ☐ **Nearly there** ☐ **Nailed it** ☐

Les projets

Qu'est-ce qu'on fera?
On ira pique-niquer dans le parc.
Ce sera génial!
Je resterai à la maison.
Je regarderai un film.
Je jouerai à des jeux vidéo/au football.
On ne fera pas de barbecue.
On mangera dans un restaurant.

Plans

What shall we do?
We'll have a picnic in the park.
That will be great!
I will stay at home.
I will watch a film.
I will play video games/football.
We won't have a barbecue.
We will eat in a restaurant.

Had a look ☐ **Nearly there** ☐ **Nailed it** ☐

Quel temps fera-t-il?

Il y aura ...
du vent
du soleil
du tonnerre
de la grêle
de la pluie
des averses
des éclairs
des éclaircies
Il fera ...

What will the weather be like?

There will be ...
wind
sun
thunder
hail
rain
showers
lightning
sunny intervals
It will be ...

beau/chaud/froid/frais
Le temps sera ...
brumeux/ensoleillé
nuageux/orageux
variable
Le ciel sera bleu/gris/couvert.
Les températures seront en baisse/en hausse.

fine/hot/cold/cool
The weather will be ...
misty/sunny
cloudy/stormy
changeable
The sky will be blue/grey/overcast.
The temperatures will be going down/going up.

Had a look ☐ **Nearly there** ☐ **Nailed it** ☐

En pleine action!

J'ai/Nous avons ...
collecté de l'argent
vendu nos vieux jeux et jouets
lavé des voitures
acheté (de la peinture)
planté des arbres
lancé une pétition en ligne
obtenu presque 2 000 signatures
écrit un article dans le journal local

Taking action

I/We have ...
collected money
sold our old games and toys
washed cars
bought (paint)
planted trees
launched an online petition
obtained nearly 2,000 signatures
written an article in the local newspaper

Had a look ☐ **Nearly there** ☐ **Nailed it** ☐

Le week-end prochain, nous irons là-bas pour ...
ramasser les déchets
nettoyer la salle
repeindre les murs
La semaine prochaine, on finira d'installer/de construire ...
un passage piéton
un panneau
une aire de jeux

Next weekend, we will go there to ...
pick up litter
clean the room
repaint the walls
Next week, we will finish installing/building ...
a pedestrian crossing
a sign
a play area

Had a look ☐ **Nearly there** ☐ **Nailed it** ☐

M 4

Extra words I should know for reading and listening activities

M 4

La géographie	*Geography*
la principauté	*principality*
le paysage	*landscape, scenery*
les Bretons (m)*	*people from Brittany*
le panorama	*panorama*
le quartier	*area*
la province	*province*
le milieu	*environment*
les gorges (f)	*gorges*
les collines (f)	*hills*

Had a look ☐ **Nearly there** ☐ **Nailed it** ☐

Les sports extrêmes	*Extreme sports*
le canyoning	*canyoning*
le saut à l'élastique	*bungee jumping*

Had a look ☐ **Nearly there** ☐ **Nailed it** ☐

Le climat	*Climate*
le changement climatique	*climate change*
le climat	*climate*
le mistral	*cold, northerly wind*
la vague de chaleur	*heatwave*
la canicule	*scorching heat, heatwave*
la tempête	*storm*
l'ouragan (m)	*hurricane*
le cyclone	*cyclone*

Had a look ☐ **Nearly there** ☐ **Nailed it** ☐

En route!	*On the road!*
la limite de vitesse	*speed limit*
les transports en commun (m)	*public transport*
les déchets (m)	*rubbish*
la circulation	*traffic*
les routes (f)	*roads*
les distributeurs de billets (m)	*cash machines*
les morts (f)	*deaths*

Had a look ☐ **Nearly there** ☐ **Nailed it** ☐

En ville	*In town*
les missions de volontariat (f)	*volunteering*
les promenades commentées (f)	*guided tours*
les stations de ski (f)	*ski resorts*
les stations balnéaires (f)	*seaside resorts*

Had a look ☐ **Nearly there** ☐ **Nailed it** ☐

Les milieux	*Environments*
défavorisé(e)	*underprivileged*
déprimant(e)	*depressing*
majestueux/-euse	*majestic*
véritable	*real*
les parfumeries (f)	*perfumeries*
les vignobles (m)	*vineyards*
les ateliers (m) de poterie (f)	*potteries*

Had a look ☐ **Nearly there** ☐ **Nailed it** ☐

Les verbes	*Verbs*
arrêter	*to stop*
causer	*to cause*
ramasser	*to collect*
collecter	*to collect*
repeindre	*to repaint*
installer	*to install*
savoir**	*to know*
connaître**	*to know*

Had a look ☐ **Nearly there** ☐ **Nailed it** ☐

Les expressions idiomatiques	*Idioms*
pas tellement mon truc!	*not really my thing!*
ma mission à moi, c'est …	*my task is to …*
un spectacle son et lumière	*a sound and light show*

Had a look ☐ **Nearly there** ☐ **Nailed it** ☐

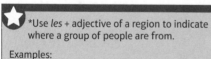

*Use *les* + adjective of a region to indicate where a group of people are from.

Examples:

Les Bretons people from Brittany

Les Provençaux people from Provence

Les Lyonnais people from the Lyon region

Les Charentais people from the Charente region

**These two verbs have the same translation but are used in different contexts:

connaître to know people, places, the existence of something and the value of something.

Je connais Lyon, c'est chouette! I know Lyon, it's great!

savoir to know how to do something, to know information you are aware of and to know of events.

Je sais nager. I know how to swim.

Words I should know for speaking and writing activities

En vacances	On holiday
l'Algérie (f)	Algeria
l'Allemagne (f)	Germany
l'Angleterre (f)	England
l'Autriche (f)	Austria
la Belgique	Belgium
la Croatie	Croatia
l'Espagne (f)	Spain
les États-Unis (m)	USA
la France	France
le Japon	Japan
le Pakistan	Pakistan
les Pays-Bas (m)	Netherlands
le pays de Galles	Wales
la Pologne	Poland
la Suisse	Switzerland

Had a look ☐ **Nearly there** ☐ **Nailed it** ☐

Normalement, je passe mes vacances en/au/à l'/aux …	Normally, I spend my holidays in …
Je vais au bord de la mer/à la campagne/à la montagne.	I go to the seaside/the countryside/the mountains.
Je voyage en train/avion/ferry/voiture.	I go by train/plane/ferry/car.
Je fais du camping.	I go camping.
Je loge dans un gîte/un hôtel/chez ma tante.	I stay in a holiday cottage/a hotel/with my aunt.
J'y vais avec ma famille/mes grand-parents/mon petit frère.	I go there with my family/my grandparents/my little brother.
C'est génial/extra/assez ennuyeux.	It's great/excellent/quite boring.
Je me lève tôt.	I get up early.
On se couche tard.	We go to bed late.
Je me repose/me prépare.	I rest/get ready.
Je m'habille.	I get dressed.
Je vais à la plage.	I go to the beach.
Je me baigne dans la mer.	I bathe/swim in the sea.
Je me promène.	I go for a walk.
Je rentre à l'hôtel.	I go back to the hotel.
Je sors au restaurant.	I go out to a restaurant.
On peut …	You can …
faire une visite de Paris	visit Paris
faire de l'escalade	go climbing
visiter les musées/monuments	visit museums/monuments
aller à la pêche/à la plage	go fishing/to the beach
jouer à la pétanque	play petanque, boules

Had a look ☐ **Nearly there** ☐ **Nailed it** ☐

Les vacances passées et futures	Holidays past and future
Tous les ans/Normalement/Tous les étés, …	Every year/Normally/Every summer, …
j'achète/je fais/je vais …	I buy/do/go …
Hier/L'année dernière/Le week-end dernier, …	Yesterday/Last year/Last weekend, …
j'ai vu/visité/acheté …	I saw/visited/bought …
je suis allé(e) à …	I went to …
L'année prochaine/Le week-end prochain/Demain, …	Next year/Next weekend/Tomorrow, …
je vais faire/prendre/aller/visiter …	I'm going to do/take/go/visit …

Had a look ☐ **Nearly there** ☐ **Nailed it** ☐

Des vacances de rêve	Dream holidays
Je logerais …	I would stay …
dans un gîte à la campagne	in a holiday cottage in the countryside
dans un hôtel 4 étoiles	in a 4-star hotel
dans une auberge de jeunesse	in a youth hostel
dans une caravane	in a caravan
dans une chambre d'hôtes	in a bed and breakfast
dans une tente, sur une île déserte	in a tent on a desert island
sur un bateau	on a boat
Je voyagerais …	I would travel …
avec mes copains/copines	with my friends
avec ma famille	with my family
avec mes parents	with my parents
avec mes grands-parents	with my grandparents
avec mon lycée	with my school
avec une organisation	with an organisation
seul(e)	alone

Had a look ☐ **Nearly there** ☐ **Nailed it** ☐

Je regarderais le coucher du soleil.	I would watch the sunset.
Je nagerais avec les poissons tropicaux.	I would swim with tropical fish.
Je ferais des randonnées.	I would go hiking.
Je ferais du canoë-kayak.	I would go canoeing.
Je me reposerais.	I would rest.
Je m'amuserais avec mes copains/copines.	I would have fun with my friends.
Je mangerais bien.	I would eat well.

M 5

Il y aurait … — *There would be …*
un café qui serait ouvert toute la nuit — *a café which would be open all night*
une salle de jeux — *a games room*
des feux d'artifice tous les soirs — *fireworks every night*
des spectacles son et lumière — *sound and light shows*
des visites guidées — *guided tours*
Il n'y aurait aucun bruit! — *There would be no noise!*
Il n'y aurait pas beaucoup d'adultes! — *There wouldn't be many adults!*
Ce serait … — *It would be …*
formidable — *tremendous*
luxueux — *luxury*
merveilleux — *wonderful*
passionnant — *exciting*
pittoresque — *picturesque*
reposant — *restful*
tranquille — *quiet*

Had a look ☐ **Nearly there** ☐ **Nailed it** ☐

À l'hôtel
At the hotel

Nous avons passé X jours dans cet hôtel/ chambre d'hôte. — *We spent X days at this hotel/bed and breakfast*
Ça s'est très bien passé. — *It all went very well.*
C'était charmant/ propre/bien situé. — *It was charming/clean/ well located.*
très pratique/pas cher/ super — *very handy/not expensive/super*
Le service était impeccable. — *The service was impeccable.*
Le Wi-Fi fonctionnait très bien. — *The Wi-Fi worked very well.*
Le petit-déjeuner était offert. — *Breakfast was included.*
Il y avait … — *There was …*
un parking tout près — *parking nearby*
un micro-onde/la climatisation dans la chambre — *a microwave/air-conditioning in the room*
Il y avait un très bon rapport qualité-prix. — *It was very good value for money.*
Nous y avons passé un super séjour. — *We had a super stay there.*

Had a look ☐ **Nearly there** ☐ **Nailed it** ☐

Je voudrais une chambre … — *I would like a room …*
pour une personne — *for one person*
pour deux personnes — *for two people*
avec un lit simple — *with a single bed*
avec un grand lit — *with a double bed*
avec une salle de bains — *with a bathroom*
avec une douche — *with a shower*
avec une vue sur la mer — *with a sea view*

Votre chambre est … — *Your room is …*
au rez-de-chaussée — *on the ground floor*
au premier/deuxième étage — *on the first/second floor*

Had a look ☐ **Nearly there** ☐ **Nailed it** ☐

Au restaurant
At the restaurant

Je préférerais une table … — *I would prefer a table …*
en terrasse/à l'intérieur — *on the terrace/inside*
Je vais prendre … — *I will have/take …*
le plat du jour/le menu à 30 euros — *the dish of the day/the 30 euros set menu*
(la soupe à la tomate) en entrée — *(the tomato soup) for a starter*
(le filet de loup de mer) comme plat principal — *(the fillet of seabass) for the main course*
(la mousse au chocolat) comme dessert — *(the chocolate mousse) for dessert*
Qu'est-ce que vous avez, comme desserts? — *What desserts do you have?*
On peut avoir l'addition, s'il vous plaît? — *Could we have the bill, please?*

Had a look ☐ **Nearly there** ☐ **Nailed it** ☐

Les prix n'étaient pas excessifs. — *The prices weren't excessive.*
C'était cher. — *It was expensive.*
L'accueil était très chaleureux. — *The welcome was very warm.*
Nous avons dû attendre plus de cinq minutes. — *We had to wait more than five minutes.*
L'ambiance était vraiment agréable. — *The ambiance was really pleasant.*
L'atmosphère était super bruyante. — *The atmosphere was very noisy.*
Le serveur/La serveuse était … — *The waiter/waitress was …*
très attentionné(e)/ médiocre — *very attentive/mediocre*
À recommander! — *To be recommended!*
Je n'y retournerai jamais! — *I will never go back there!*
un couteau — *a knife*
une cuillère — *a spoon*
une fourchette — *a fork*
une serviette — *a napkin*

Had a look ☐ **Nearly there** ☐ **Nailed it** ☐

Les plats
The dishes

les entrées (f) — *starters*
les brochettes (f) de crevettes (f) — *prawn skewers*
les escargots (m) — *snails*
la soupe à la tomate — *tomato soup*
la tarte à l'oignon — *onion tart*
les plats principaux (m) — *main dishes*

'épaule (f) d'agneau	lamb shoulder
la cuisse de canard	duck leg
le gratin dauphinois	dauphinoise potatoes
les lasagnes (f) végétariennes	vegetarian lasagne
le loup de mer	sea bass
le poulet basquaise	Basque-style chicken
le rôti de veau	roast veal
les desserts (m)	desserts
la crème brûlée	crème brûlée
la mousse au chocolat	chocolate mousse
le roulé au chocolat	chocolate roll
le sorbet	sorbet
la tarte au citron	lemon tart
la tarte aux pommes	apple tart

Had a look ☐ **Nearly there** ☐ **Nailed it** ☐

En route! *On the road!*

Si j'avais le choix, pour aller …	If I had the choice, to go …
en Inde/Russie/Chine	to India/Russia/China
au Sénégal/Vietnam/Brésil	to Senegal/Vietnam/Brazil
… je voyagerais …	… I would travel …
en car/train/avion	by coach/train/plane
à moto	by motorbike
… car c'est/ce n'est pas …	… because it is (not) …
rapide/confortable/pratique	quick/comfortable/practical
une aventure/la classe	an adventure/cool
bon pour l'environnement	good for the environment
ennuyeux	boring
fatigant	tiring
cher	expensive
un billet	a ticket
un aller simple	a single
un aller-retour	a return
en première classe	in first class
en deuxième classe	in second class
les horaires	travel time(s)
le guichet	ticket office
le quai	platform
la salle d'attente	waiting room

Had a look ☐ **Nearly there** ☐ **Nailed it** ☐

Acheter les souvenirs *Buying souvenirs*

Je pense acheter (ce tagine).	I'm thinking of buying (this tagine).
Qu'est-ce que tu en penses?	What do you think of it?
Que penses-tu de (cette théière)?	What do you think of (this teapot)?
Je crois que je vais acheter (ces bijoux).	I think I'm going to buy (this jewellery).
Je veux acheter (un foulard).	I want to buy (a scarf).
Tu préfères celui-ci ou celui-là?	Do you prefer this one or that one?
Je cherche (une lanterne) pour (ma sœur).	I'm looking for (a lantern) for (my sister).
Je prends celle-ci ou celle-là?	Shall I take this one or that one?
J'ai envie de m'acheter des (gants).	I feel like buying some (gloves).
Tu trouves celles-ci comment?	What do you think of these?
Je déteste faire du shopping.	I hate going shopping.
Je suis accro au shopping.	I'm addicted to shopping.

Had a look ☐ **Nearly there** ☐ **Nailed it** ☐

C'était catastrophique! *It was catastrophic!*

Avant de partir, j'avais …	Before leaving I had …
réservé mon billet d'avion	booked my plane ticket
fait ma valise/des recherches	packed my case/done some research
découvert/décidé que …	discovered/decided that …
tout préparé	prepared everything
J'étais allé(e) à l'agence de voyages.	I had gone to the travel agent's.
Mais/Pourtant …	But/However …
je me suis cassé la jambe	I broke my leg
j'ai oublié mon passeport	I forgot my passport
j'ai raté l'avion	I missed the plane
j'ai pris un coup de soleil affreux	I got terribly sunburnt
le camping-car est tombé en panne	the camper van broke down
on m'a volé mon sac à main	my handbag was stolen
Alors/Donc …	So …
j'ai dû aller au commissariat/à l'hôpital/chez le médecin	I had to go to the police station/hospital/doctor's
Quelle horreur!	How awful!
J'étais triste.	I was sad.
On était bien déçus.	We were really disappointed.

Had a look ☐ **Nearly there** ☐ **Nailed it** ☐

M 5

M
5

Extra words I should know for reading and listening activities

Les souvenirs de vacances	*Holiday memories*
le tagine	*Moroccan cooking pot*
la théière	*teapot*
les poissons tropicaux (m)	*tropical fish*
les créatures (f)	*creatures*

Had a look ☐ **Nearly there** ☐ **Nailed it** ☐

En vacances	*On holiday!*
les vacances de neige (f)	*winter holidays*
l'île déserte (f)	*desert island*
le coin de paradis	*corner of paradise*
dans un beau cadre	*in a beautiful area*
à l'intérieur	*inside*
le parc naturel	*nature/national park*
le coup de soleil	*sunburn*
les marchands (m)	*shopkeepers*
l'auberge de jeunesse (f)	*youth hostel*
la climatisation	*air-conditioning*
le pourboire	*tip*
l'hôtel 4 étoiles (m)	*4 star hotel*
la formule demi-pension	*half-board*
en montgolfière (f)	*in a hot air ballon*
le Wi-Fi	*wi-fi*

Had a look ☐ **Nearly there** ☐ **Nailed it** ☐

Les activités de vacances	*Holiday activities*
installer	*to put in*
emporter	*to take*
vomir	*to be sick*
être à couper le souffle	*to be breath-taking*
profiter de	*to make the most of*
se baigner	*to swim*
endormir	*to fall asleep*
rater	*to miss (bus, etc.)*
faire des recherches	*to research*
rapporter	*to bring back*
essayer	*to try*
tomber en panne	*to break down*
voler	*to steal*
hurler	*to scream*
loger	*to stay*
en regardant …	*while watching …*

Had a look ☐ **Nearly there** ☐ **Nailed it** ☐

Les expressions idiomatiques	*Idioms*
c'est une bonne affaire?	*is it a good deal/bargain?*
qu'est-que c'était cher!	*it was so expensive!*
chez le médecin	*at the doctor's*
à recommander!	*I would recommend it!*
le petit-déjeuner était offert!*	*breakfast was included!*

Had a look ☐ **Nearly there** ☐ **Nailed it** ☐

> ⭐ *Offert* really means 'offered' but it conveys the idea of 'given away with' something, so here breakfast is given away with the stay in the hotel!
>
> Another example:
>
> *Achetez deux jeux et le troisième est offert!* Buy two games and the third is free/given away!

Words I should know for speaking and writing activities

Les matières	School subjects
le commerce	business studies
le dessin	art
les arts plastiques (m)	fine art
le français	French
le latin	Latin
la biologie/les sciences de la vie et de la terre	biology
la chimie	chemistry
la géographie	geography
la musique	music
la physique/les sciences physiques	physics
la religion	religious studies
la sociologie	sociology
la technologie	design and technology
l'allemand (m)	German
l'anglais (m)	English

Had a look ☐   **Nearly there** ☐   **Nailed it** ☐

l'art dramatique (m)	drama
l'économie (f)	economics
l'éducation physique et sportive/l'EPS (f)	PE
l'espagnol (m)	Spanish
l'étude des médias (f)	media studies
l'histoire (f)	history
l'histoire-géo (f)	humanities (history and geography, studied together in France)
l'informatique (f)	ICT
l'instruction civique (f)	citizenship
l'italien (m)	Italian
les arts ménagers (m)	home technology
les maths (f)	maths

Had a look ☐   **Nearly there** ☐   **Nailed it** ☐

Mon collège — My school

Mercredi, à 11h15, j'ai histoire-géo.	I have humanities at 11:15 a.m. on Wednesday.
J'ai (deux) heures de (musique) par semaine.	I have (two) hours of (music) per week.
Il n'y a pas de cours de ... dans mon emploi du temps.	There are no ... lessons in my timetable.
J'apprends (deux) langues vivantes.	I learn (two) foreign languages.
Mes cours finissent à (16h00) tous les jours.	My lessons finish at (4:00 p.m.) every day.
Je n'ai pas cours (le mercredi après-midi).	I don't have lessons (on Wednesday afternoon).
Ma matière préférée est ...	My favourite subject is ...
J'adore/j'aime/je n'aime pas/je déteste ...	I love/like/don't like/hate ...
Je trouve ...	I find ...

Had a look ☐   **Nearly there** ☐   **Nailed it** ☐

Je pense que ... est/sont ...	I think that ... is ...
intéressant(e)(s)	interesting
passionnant(e)(s)	exciting
ennuyeux/-euse(s)	boring
... parce que/qu' ...	... because ...
c'est facile/fascinant/difficile/utile/inutile	it's easy/fascinating/difficult/useful/useless
Je suis fort(e)/faible/doué(e) en ...	I am strong/weak/gifted in ...
Le/La prof est bon(ne)/sympa/marrant(e)/sévère/gentil(le)/impatient(e).	The teacher is good/nice/funny/strict/kind/impatient.
On a trop de devoirs.	We have too much homework.

Had a look ☐   **Nearly there** ☐   **Nailed it** ☐

Mon bahut — My school

Comment s'appelle ton collège?	What's your school called?
Mon collège s'appelle ...	My school is called ...
C'est quelle sorte de collège?	What sort of school is it?
C'est un collège mixte pour les élèves de onze à seize ans.	It's a mixed school for pupils from 11 to 16.
Il y a combien d'élèves?	How many pupils are there?
Il y a 750 élèves et quarante-cinq professeurs.	There are 750 pupils and 45 teachers.
Quelles sont les horaires du collège?	What are the school hours?
Les cours commencent à 8h30.	Lessons start at 8:30 a.m.
La récré est à 10h15 et dure quinze minutes.	Break is at 10:15 a.m. and lasts 15 minutes.
On a une heure et demie pour le déjeuner.	We have an hour and a half for lunch.
Les cours finissent à 16 heures.	Lessons finish at 4:00 p.m.

Had a look ☐   **Nearly there** ☐   **Nailed it** ☐

Il y a combien de cours par jour?	How many lessons are there per day?
Il y a sept cours de cinquante-cinq minutes par jour.	There are seven lessons of 55 minutes per day.
Le mercredi après-midi, il n'y a pas cours.	There are no lessons on Wednesday afternoon.
Quelles matières étudies-tu?	What subjects do you study?
J'étudie douze matières dont ...	I study 12 subjects, including ...
Toutes mes matières sont obligatoires.	All my subjects are compulsory.
Quelle est ta matière préférée?	What is your favourite subject?

M 6

Ma matière préférée, c'est (les arts ménagers) car …	My favourite subject is (home technology) because …
J'adore (cuisiner) car …	I love (cooking) because …
je suis doué(e) pour ça	I'm talented at that
Comment sont les professeurs?	What are your teachers like?
Les profs sont sympa/ sévères.	The teachers are nice/ strict.
Qu'est-ce que tu penses de ton collège?	What do you think of your school?
Je trouve que/qu' …	I find that …
les journées sont trop longues	the days are too long
on a trop de contrôles	we have too many tests
les profs sont excellents	the teachers are excellent

Had a look ☐ **Nearly there** ☐ **Nailed it** ☐

L'école chez nous, l'école chez vous
School here and with you

En Angleterre/Écosse/ Irlande du Nord …	In England/Scotland/ Northern Ireland …
Au pays de Galles …	In Wales …
on va à l'école de … ans à … ans	we go to school from … to … years old
l'école commence à … heures et finit à … heures	school starts at … and finishes at …
on porte un uniforme scolaire/ses propres vêtements	we wear a school uniform/our own clothes
on achète ses propres stylos et règles	we buy our own pens and rulers
on ne redouble pas	we don't repeat the year
on étudie …	we study …
Mais en France/au Canada/au Mali …	But in France/Canada/ Mali …
ils vont …	they go …
l'école commence …	school starts …
ils portent …	they wear …
ils achètent …	they buy …
ils (ne) redoublent (pas)	they (don't) repeat the year
ils étudient …	they study …
Je préfère le système (anglais/français)	I prefer the (English/ French) system
parce que …	because …
les horaires sont plus raisonnables	the hours are more sensible
l'uniforme scolaire est pratique/inutile	school uniform is practical/useless
l'école fournit l'équipement	school provides the equipment
le redoublement (n')est (pas) une bonne idée	repeating the year is (not) a good idea
on (n')étudie (pas) …	we/they (don't) study …

Had a look ☐ **Nearly there** ☐ **Nailed it** ☐

Le règlement scolaire
School rules

Dans cette école, il faut …	In this school, you must …
être à l'heure	be on time
faire ses devoirs	do your homework
porter l'uniforme scolaire	wear school uniform
Il ne faut pas …	You must not …
manquer les cours	miss lessons
tricher pendant un contrôle	cheat in a test
Il est interdit de/d' …	It is forbidden to …
mâcher du chewing-gum	chew gum
utiliser son portable en classe	use your mobile in class
porter des bijoux/ des piercings/trop de maquillage	wear jewellery/piercings/ too much make-up
harceler d'autres élèves	bully other pupils
sortir de l'école pendant l'heure du déjeuner	leave school during the lunch hour

Had a look ☐ **Nearly there** ☐ **Nailed it** ☐

Je trouve ça …	I find that …
raisonnable	reasonable, sensible
logique	logical
juste/injuste	fair/unfair
ridicule/frustrant	ridiculous/frustrating
… parce que/car …	… because …
c'est/ce n'est pas dangereux	it's (not) dangerous
il faut protéger les jeunes	you must protect young people
on n'est pas des bébés	we're not babies
il faut respecter les autres	you must respect others
la mode n'a pas de place à l'école	fashion has no place at school
c'est/ce n'est pas important	it's (not) important
l'école, c'est pour apprendre	school is for learning
J'ai eu une heure de retenue/de colle.	I had an hour of detention.
J'ai dû copier des lignes.	I had to write lines.

Had a look ☐ **Nearly there** ☐ **Nailed it** ☐

Des conseils pour être en bonne santé
Advice for being healthy

se concentrer en classe	to concentrate in class
se coucher tôt	to go to bed early
se détendre	to relax
dormir huit heures par nuit	to sleep eight hours per night
éteindre les écrans	to turn off screens
être en bonne forme physique	to be in good physical shape

M 6

se faire de nouveaux amis	to make new friends
faire de la méditation ou du yoga	to do meditation or yoga
faire une activité sportive	to do a sport/sporting activity
manger équilibré	to eat a balanced diet
participer à la chorale	to participate in the choir
profiter des sorties scolaires	to make the most of school trips
se reposer	to rest
respirer	to breathe
le corps	the body
l'esprit (m)	the mind
le sommeil	sleep
les matières grasses (f)	fat(s)

Had a look ☐ **Nearly there** ☐ **Nailed it** ☐

Ce que je fais / What I do

Je mange sainement.	I eat healthily.
J'essaie de manger cinq portions de fruits et de légumes par jour.	I try to eat five portions of fruit and vegetables per day.
Je suis végétarien(ne).	I'm a vegetarian.
Je mange rarement des bonbons.	I rarely eat sweets.
Je fais attention à ce que je bois.	I am careful about what I drink.
Je ne bois pas de boissons gazeuses.	I don't drink fizzy drinks.

Had a look ☐ **Nearly there** ☐ **Nailed it** ☐

Quand et comment? / When and how?

calmement	calmly
dur	hard
également	equally, also
énormément	enormously, hugely
facilement	easily
heureusement	fortunately
lentement	slowly
mieux	better
rarement	rarely
récemment	recently
régulièrement	regularly
sainement	healthily
suffisamment	enough, sufficiently
uniquement	only

Had a look ☐ **Nearly there** ☐ **Nailed it** ☐

Les vices / Vices

boire de l'alcool	to drink alcohol
se droguer	to take drugs
fumer (des cigarettes, du cannabis)	to smoke (cigarettes, cannabis)
avoir mal à la tête	to have a headache
s'isoler	to isolate yourself

souffrir de changements d'humeur	to suffer from mood swings
ivre	drunk
je suis accro à …	I'm addicted to …

Had a look ☐ **Nearly there** ☐ **Nailed it** ☐

Les opinions / Opinions

C'est un gaspillage d'argent.	It's a waste of money.
Ça coûte très cher.	It costs a lot./It's very expensive.
C'est mauvais pour la santé.	It's bad for your health.
On risque d'avoir un cancer (des poumons, du foie) ou d'autres problèmes.	You risk getting (lung, liver) cancer or other problems.
C'est dangereux.	It's dangerous.
C'est nocif.	It's harmful.
On devient facilement accro.	You become addicted easily.
On peut vite devenir dépendant.	You can quickly become dependent.
Si on fume, on sent la fumée.	If you smoke, you smell of smoke.
Ça pue.	It stinks.
Ça me donne confiance.	It gives me confidence.
Ça m'aide dans les situations sociales.	It helps me in social situations.
Je ne veux pas grossir.	I don't want to put on weight.

M 6

Had a look ☐ **Nearly there** ☐ **Nailed it** ☐

En échange / On an exchange

Pourquoi faire un échange scolaire?	Why go on a school exchange?
On se fait de nouveaux amis.	You make new friends.
On améliore ses compétences en langue.	You improve your language skills.
On habite chez une famille d'une culture différente.	You live with a family from another culture.
On visite un nouveau pays ou une nouvelle région.	You visit a new country or region.
On apprécie non seulement les différences mais aussi les similarités entre nos vies.	You appreciate not only the differences, but also the similarities between our lives.

Had a look ☐ **Nearly there** ☐ **Nailed it** ☐

Extra words I should know for reading and listening activities

Les personnes / *People*

le/la surveillant(e)	supervisor
l'internat (m)	boarding school
le/la collégien(ne)	high school student (up to yr10)
le/la correspondant(e)	penfriend

Had a look ☐ **Nearly there** ☐ **Nailed it** ☐

Les problèmes / *Problems*

les matières grasses (f)	fats
la cigarette*	smoking
la fumée	smoke
le cancer	cancer
le gaspillage d'argent	waste of money

Had a look ☐ **Nearly there** ☐ **Nailed it** ☐

La vie / *Life*

facultatif/-ve	optional
admis(e)	admitted
voisin(e)	neighbouring
payé par	paid by
nocif/-ve	harmful
addictif/-ve	addictive
réel(le)	real
virtuel(le)	virtual

Had a look ☐ **Nearly there** ☐ **Nailed it** ☐

Les activités au collège / *School activities*

les arts plastiques (m)	fine arts
la musculation	body building
l'entraînement (m)	training
l'instruction civique (f)	citizenship
le progrès	progress
la maternelle	pre-school/nursery school
le bac	A levels
le contrôle	test
la pièce de théâtre	play
la chorale	choir
la marche rapide	power-walking
le chant	singing
le sommeil	sleep
la scolarité	schooling
la mémoire	memory
les compétences (f)	skills

Had a look ☐ **Nearly there** ☐ **Nailed it** ☐

Les problèmes au collège / *School problems*

sécher les cours/ manquer les cours	to skip lessons/to truant
en quittant …	on leaving …
mâcher*	to chew
harceler	to bully
tricher	to cheat
stresser	to stress
améliorer	to improve
manger équilibré	to eat a balanced diet
rester en forme	to keep fit

Had a look ☐ **Nearly there** ☐ **Nailed it** ☐

> ★ *Watch out for 'false friends' such as *la cigarette* and *mâcher*. Learn as many of them as you can so that they don't catch you out in the exam!
>
> Another example of a false friend is the verb *redoubler*. This actually means 'to redo another school year', not 'to double again'.

M 6

Words I should know for speaking and writing activities

Les professions	Jobs
Ma mère/Mon père est ...	My mum/dad is a(n) ...
Je voudrais être ...	I would like to be a(n) ...
acteur/-rice	actor/actress
agent de police	policeman/woman
agriculteur/-rice	farmer
architecte	architect
boucher/-ère	butcher
boulanger/-ère	baker
caissier/-ère	cashier
coiffeur/-euse	hairdresser
créateur/-rice de mode	fashion designer
dentiste	dentist
directeur/-rice	director
électricien(ne)	electrician
employé(e) de bureau	office worker

Had a look ☐   **Nearly there** ☐   **Nailed it** ☐

facteur/-rice	postman/postwoman
fonctionnaire	civil servant
infirmier/-ère	nurse
informaticien(ne)	computer scientist
ingénieur(e)	engineer
journaliste	journalist
maçon(ne)	builder
mécanicien(ne)	mechanic
médecin	doctor
professeur	teacher
secrétaire	secretary
serveur/-euse	waiter/waitress
soldat	soldier
steward/hôtesse de l'air	flight attendant
vendeur/-euse	sales assistant
vétérinaire	vet

Had a look ☐   **Nearly there** ☐   **Nailed it** ☐

J'adore (la campagne).	I love (the countryside).
Je suis passionné(e) par (la loi et la justice).	I'm passionate about (the law and justice).
Je suis fort(e) en (maths).	I'm good at (maths).
Je suis (courageux/-euse).	I am (brave).
(Voyager), c'est ma passion.	(Travelling) is my passion.
(Les avions) me fascinent.	(Planes) fascinate me.
Je préférerais travailler (en plein air).	I would prefer to work (outdoors).
Je voudrais travailler avec (des enfants).	I would like to work with (children).
Je voudrais/J'aimerais travailler comme ...	I would like to work as ...
Je veux être ...	I want to be ...

Had a look ☐   **Nearly there** ☐   **Nailed it** ☐

L'orientation	Career paths
Dans quel secteur voudrais-tu travailler?	In which area would you like to work?
l'audiovisuel et les médias	audiovisual and media
l'informatique et les télécommunications	IT and telecommunications
l'hôtellerie et la restauration	hotel and catering
les arts et la culture	arts and culture
le commerce	business
le sport et les loisirs	sport and leisure
la médecine et la santé	medicine and health
les sciences et les technologies	science and technology
Ça m'intéresserait de travailler dans ...	I would be interested in working in ...
Mon rêve serait de faire carrière dans ...	My dream would be to have a career in ...
Mon ambition/Mon but est de trouver un poste dans ...	My ambition/aim is to find a job in ...

Had a look ☐   **Nearly there** ☐   **Nailed it** ☐

M 7

Le secteur/L'orientation qui m'attire/m'intéresse (le plus), c'est ...	The sector/career path that attracts/ interests me (the most) is ...
L'important pour moi est d'avoir un métier bien payé.	The important thing for me is to have a well-paid job.
Le plus important est de ...	The most important thing is to ...
faire quelque chose de satisfaisant/stimulant/ gratifiant/d'intéressant	do something satisfying/ stimulating/rewarding/ interesting
faire quelque chose pour améliorer la société/aider les autres	do something to improve society/help others
Le salaire a moins d'importance/est très important pour moi.	The salary is less/very important to me.
À mon avis, c'est un secteur d'avenir.	In my opinion, it's an area with prospects.
Je suis ... depuis (trois) ans.	I have been a ... for (three) years.
C'est un métier (stimulant).	It's a (stimulating) job.

Had a look ☐   **Nearly there** ☐   **Nailed it** ☐

La chose qui me plaît le plus, c'est ...	What I like best is ...
L'inconvénient, c'est que ...	The disadvantage is that ...
les horaires sont très longs	the hours are very long
c'est fatigant	it's tiring

Had a look ☐   **Nearly there** ☐   **Nailed it** ☐

Le mieux/pire, c'est …	The best/worst thing is …
Je suis assez satisfait(e) de mon travail.	I'm quite satisfied with my job.
Avant, j'étais/je travaillais comme …	In the past, I was/worked as …
C'était affreux/stressant/mieux/pire.	It was awful/stressful/better/worse.
C'était mal payé.	It was badly paid.
Le travail était monotone.	The work was monotonous.
Il n'y avait aucune possibilité d'avancement.	There was no chance of promotion.
Je m'entendais mal avec mon patron.	I didn't get on well with my boss.
J'ai décidé de (suivre une formation).	I decided to (take a course).
Maintenant, je suis diplômé(e).	Now I am qualified.
Mon nouveau boulot est (plus créatif).	My new job is (more creative).
Mes collègues sont tous très sympa.	My colleagues are all very nice.

Had a look ☐ **Nearly there** ☐ **Nailed it** ☐

Les ambitions — *Ambitions*

Avant de continuer mes études, …	Before I continue my studies …
Après avoir terminé mes examens, …	After having finished my exams …
Après avoir quitté le collège, …	After having left school …
Plus tard/Un jour, …	Later on/One day …
Je veux/J'aimerais/Je préférerais/J'espère	I want/I would like/I would prefer/I hope
J'ai envie de/d' …	I want to …
J'ai l'intention de/d' …	I intend to …
Mon rêve serait de/d' …	My dream would be to …
aller à l'université/à la fac	go to university
entrer en apprentissage	do an apprenticeship
faire du bénévolat/travail bénévole	do charity/voluntary work
prendre une année sabbatique	take a gap year
J'espère me marier/me pacser.	I hope to get married/register a civil partnership.
J'ai l'intention de faire le tour du monde.	I intend to travel round the world.
Mon but est de fonder une famille.	My aim is to start a family.
Je ne veux pas avoir d'enfants.	I don't want to have children.
Je n'ai aucune intention de m'installer avec mon copain/ma copine.	I have no intention of moving in with my boyfriend/girlfriend.

Had a look ☐ **Nearly there** ☐ **Nailed it** ☐

Au téléphone — *On the telephone*

Allô?	Hello?
Je voudrais parler avec …	I would like to talk to …
Sa ligne est occupée.	His/Her line is busy.
Est-ce que je peux laisser un message?	Can I leave a message?
Je vais vous transférer vers sa messagerie vocale.	I will transfer you to his/her voicemail.
Ne quittez pas.	Stay on the line.
Je vous le passe.	I'll pass you over to him/her.
Je peux vous être utile?	Can I help you/be of help?
Au revoir!	Goodbye!

Had a look ☐ **Nearly there** ☐ **Nailed it** ☐

Un entretien d'embauche — *A job interview*

Enchanté(e).	Pleased to meet you.
Asseyez-vous.	Sit down.
Parlez-moi un peu de ce que vous faites actuellement.	Talk to me a little bit about what you are doing at the moment.
Actuellement, je suis (au lycée).	At the moment, I am (in sixth form college).
Je suis en train de (préparer le baccalauréat/mes examens de GCSE).	I am in the middle of (preparing to take my baccalauréat/my GCSE exams).
Quelles matières étudiez-vous?	What subjects are you studying?
J'étudie (huit) matières, dont (l'EPS).	I'm studying (eight) subjects, including (PE).
Qu'est-ce que vous ferez après vos examens?	What will you do after your exams?

Had a look ☐ **Nearly there** ☐ **Nailed it** ☐

Mon boulot dans le tourisme — *My job in tourism*

Je suis étudiant(e) en …	I am studying …
J'apprends à devenir …	I'm learning to become …
Il y a six mois, j'ai commencé à travailler dans/chez/en …	Six months ago I started work in/with …
Je voudrais travailler à plein temps dans (le tourisme).	I would like to work full-time in (tourism).
Lorsque j'étais plus jeune, je rêvais d'être (infirmier/-ière).	When I was younger, I dreamed of being a (nurse).
J'ai décidé de changer d'orientation à cause de …	I decide to change direction because of …

Had a look ☐ **Nearly there** ☐ **Nailed it** ☐

Mon travail consiste à (accueillir les clients).	*My work involves (welcoming clients).*
Je m'occupe aussi (des réservations).	*I also take care of (reservations).*

Had a look ☐   **Nearly there** ☐   **Nailed it** ☐

Je vends (des billets).	*I sell (tickets).*
Je suis passionné(e) par mon travail.	*I am passionate about my job.*
J'apprécie surtout (le contact avec les gens).	*I particularly enjoy (dealing with people).*
Le seul inconvénient de mon métier, c'est que …	*The only disadvantage of my job is that …*
Pour faire ce métier, il faut …	*To do this job you have to …*
être souriant	*smile*
savoir parler d'autres langues	*know how to speak other languages*
Plus tard/Quand je serai diplômé(e), …	*Later on/When I am qualified …*
je partirai en vacances	*I will go on holiday*
j'essaierai d'apprendre le japonais	*I will try to learn Japanese*

Had a look ☐   **Nearly there** ☐   **Nailed it** ☐

M
7

Extra words I should know for reading and listening activities

Le travail	Work
l'hôtellerie (f)	*hotel business*
la restauration	*catering*
l'orientation (f)	*careers advice*
l'horaire (m)	*timetable*
la possibilité	*possibility*
la formation	*training*
le boulot	*job*
l'année sabbatique (f)	*sabbatical/gap year*
la licence	*degree*
la sécurité	*security*
le respect	*respect*
la maîtrise	*expertise*
l'inconvénient (m)	*disadvantage*
la lettre de motivation	*covering letter*
l'encadrement (m)	*training*
la fac	*uni*

Had a look ☐ **Nearly there** ☐ **Nailed it** ☐

Les descriptions des emplois	Work-related descriptions
diplômé(e)	*qualified*
stimulant(e)	*stimulating*
ancien(e)*	*former, ancient*
pire	*worse*
mal payé(e)	*badly paid*
monotone	*monotonous*
affreux/-euse	*awful*
enrichissant(e)	*enriching*

de mauvaise humeur	*in a bad mood*
créatif/-ve	*creative*
autonome	*independent*
apprenti(e)	*trainee, apprentice*
moi-même	*myself*
à plein temps	*full-time*

Had a look ☐ **Nearly there** ☐ **Nailed it** ☐

Les activités au travail	Work-related activities
se débrouiller	*to cope, to manage*
garantir	*to guarantee*
remplir	*to fill*
s'adapter à	*to adapt to*
s'organiser	*to get organised*
entraîner	*to train*
accueillir	*to welcome*
prendre en charge	*to take charge*
animer	*to lead/facilitate activities*
s'occuper de	*to look after*
garder les enfants	*to babysit*
Que faire?	*What do I do?*
poser sa candidature	*to apply for (a job)*
après avoir/être + past participle**	*after having …*

Had a look ☐ **Nearly there** ☐ **Nailed it** ☐

*Remember that some adjectives like *ancien* change their meaning depending on where they go in relation to the noun.

Examples:

un ancien collège a former school

une ville ancienne an ancient town

**Use this structure to add a different dimension to your phrases in the past tense.

Example:

Après avoir posé ma candidature … After having applied for my job …

Remember to agree the past participle with the subject when using *être*.

Après être rentrée à la maison, la femme a ouvert les fenêtres. After having returned home, the woman opened the windows.

Words I should know for speaking and writing activities

Ce qui me préoccupe — *What worries me*

Ce qui est important pour moi dans la vie, c'est d'abord …	*The most important thing to me in life is above all …*
Ensuite, c'est …	*Then it's …*
le sport	*sport*
la musique	*music*
ma santé	*my health*
ma famille	*my family*
l'argent (m)	*money*
mes études	*my studies*
mes animaux	*my pets*
mes amis	*my friends*
Ce qui me préoccupe/ m'inquiète (le plus), c'est …	*What worries me (the most) is …*
l'état (m) de la Terre	*the state of the Earth*
le réchauffement climatique	*global warming*
la pauvreté dans le monde	*world poverty*
l'injustice (f)	*injustice*
l'environnement (m)	*the environment*
les sans-abri	*homeless people*
les personnes qui sont emprisonnées à tort	*people who have been wrongly imprisoned*
les enfants qui n'ont pas à manger	*starving children*

Had a look ☐ **Nearly there** ☐ **Nailed it** ☐

On peut/Il est possible de …	*You can/It's possible to …*
parrainer un enfant en Afrique	*sponsor a child in Africa*
faire un don à une association caritative	*donate to a charity*
faire du bénévolat	*do voluntary work*
Il faut …	*We must …*
lutter contre la faim	*fight against hunger/ famine*
lancer des pétitions	*launch petitions*
écrire à son/sa député(e)	*write to our MP*
participer à des manifestations	*take part in demonstrations*
agir maintenant	*act now*
faire des campagnes de sensibilisation	*carry out campaigns to raise awareness*
Il ne faut pas ignorer (ces gens).	*We must not ignore (these people).*

Had a look ☐ **Nearly there** ☐ **Nailed it** ☐

Notre planète — *Our planet*

Le plus grand problème pour la planète, c'est …	*The greatest problem for the planet is …*

le changement climatique	*climate change*
le déboisement	*deforestation*
la destruction de la couche d'ozone	*the destruction of the ozone layer*
la destruction des forêts tropicales	*the destruction of tropical rainforests*
la disparition des espèces	*species dying out*
la guerre	*war*
le manque d'eau douce	*the lack of fresh water*
la pollution de l'air	*air pollution*
la sécheresse	*drought*
la surpopulation	*overpopulation*
un incendie (m)	*a fire*
une fuite de pétrole	*an oil spill*
des inondations (f)	*flooding, floods*
un tremblement de terre	*an earthquake*
un typhon	*a typhoon*

Had a look ☐ **Nearly there** ☐ **Nailed it** ☐

Protéger l'environnement — *Protecting the environment*

Que devrait-on faire pour sauver notre planète?	*What should we do to save our planet?*
Actuellement, je ne fais pas grand-chose pour protéger l'environnement.	*Currently, I don't do much to protect the environment.*
Je fais déjà pas mal de choses.	*I already do quite a lot.*
Je pourrais/On devrait …	*I could/We ought to …*
trier les déchets	*separate the rubbish*
faire du compost à la maison	*make compost at home*
éteindre les appareils électriques et la lumière en quittant une pièce	*turn off appliances and the light when leaving a room*
baisser le chauffage et mettre un pull	*turn down the heating and put on a sweater*
utiliser du papier recyclé	*use recycled paper*
éviter les produits jetables	*avoid disposable products*
acheter des produits verts	*buy green products*

Had a look ☐ **Nearly there** ☐ **Nailed it** ☐

privilégier les produits bio	*where possible, choose organic products*
utiliser les transports en commun	*use public transport*
favoriser le covoiturage	*encourage car-sharing*

M 8

aller au collège à vélo	go to school by bike
refuser les sacs en plastique	turn down plastic bags
apporter une bouteille d'eau au lieu de prendre un gobelet jetable	carry a bottle of water instead of using disposable cups
récupérer l'eau de pluie pour arroser le jardin	collect rainwater for watering the garden
fermer le robinet pendant qu'on se lave les dents	turn off the tap when cleaning teeth
boire l'eau du robinet	drink tap water
prendre une douche au lieu de prendre un bain	shower instead of taking a bath
tirer la chasse d'eau moins fréquemment	flush the toilet less frequently
faire plus	do more

Had a look ☐ **Nearly there** ☐ **Nailed it** ☐

D'où vient ton tee-shirt? / Where does your T-shirt come from?

Les produits pas chers sont souvent fabriqués dans des conditions de travail inacceptables.	Cheap products are often made in unacceptable working conditions.
Les ouvriers sont sous-payés.	The workers are underpaid.
Leur journée de travail est trop longue.	Their working day is too long.
Si un produit est bon marché, je ne l'achète pas.	If a product is cheap, I don't buy it.
Trop de travailleurs sont exploités/exposés à des risques.	Too many workers are exploited/exposed to risks.

Had a look ☐ **Nearly there** ☐ **Nailed it** ☐

À mon avis, on devrait …	In my opinion, people should …
boycotter les grandes marques qui ne respectent pas leurs ouvriers	boycott big brands that don't respect their workers
forcer les grandes marques à garantir un salaire minimum	force big brands to guarantee a minimum wage
acheter des habits issus du commerce équitable	buy fairly traded clothes
acheter des vêtements fabriqués en France	buy clothes made in France
réfléchir à l'impact sur l'environnement	think about the impact on the environment
essayer de respecter l'homme et l'environnement à la fois	try to respect mankind and the environment at the same time

Had a look ☐ **Nearly there** ☐ **Nailed it** ☐

Faire du bénévolat / Volunteering

Ça me permet d'élargir mes compétences.	It allows me to expand my skills.
Ça me donne plus confiance en moi.	It gives me more confidence in myself/ makes me feel more confident.
Ça me donne le sentiment d'être utile.	It makes me feel useful.
C'est important de participer à la vie en société.	It's important to participate in society.
On a la responsabilité d'aider les autres et de ne pas se focaliser sur soi-même.	We have a responsibility to help others and not focus on ourselves.
Je travaille …	I work …
sur un stand d'Oxfam	on an Oxfam stand
dans un refuge pour les animaux	in an animal sanctuary
Je fais partie de l'organisation X.	I'm a member of X.
Je rends visite à une personne âgée.	I visit an elderly person.
Je participe à des projets de conservation.	I take part in conservation projets.
J'aide des enfants du primaire à faire leurs devoirs.	I help primary school children to do their homework.
Je soigne les animaux.	I look after/treat animals.
Je soutiens les SDF.	I support homeless people.
On s'adresse aux …	We appeal to …
sensibiliser	to raise awareness
prendre conscience de	to become aware of
soigner	to look after, to treat
accueillir	to welcome
affronter	to face, to confront
soutenir	to support

Had a look ☐ **Nearly there** ☐ **Nailed it** ☐

Les grands événements / Big events

Un avantage de cet événement, c'est que …	An advantage of this event is that …
D'un côté, ça …	On the one hand, it …
En plus, ça …	What's more/Moreover, it …
met en avant la culture	promotes the culture
met en avant la ville hôte	promotes the host city
crée un sentiment de fierté nationale	creates a sense of national pride
permet aux gens de passer un bon moment	allows people to have a good time

ncourage la pratique du sport	*encourages participation in sport*
nit les gens	*unites people*
onne des modèles aux eunes	*gives young people role models*
rée du travail	*creates jobs*
ttire des touristes	*attracts tourists*

Had a look ☐ **Nearly there** ☐ **Nailed it** ☐

Cependant, ...	*However, ...*
n inconvénient, 'est que ...	*a disadvantage is that ...*
)'un autre côté, ...	*On the other hand, ...*
Par ailleurs, ...	*What's more, ...*
es ouvriers qui construisent les stades ont souvent exploités	*the workers who build the stadiums are often exploited*
es prix augmentent	*prices rise*
a ville hôte est souvent endettée après 'événement	*the host city is often in debt after the event*
ça laisse une empreinte carbone très importante	*it leaves a major carbon footprint*
'estime/Je trouve/Je suis persuadé(e) que/ qu' ...	*I reckon/find/am persuaded that ...*
l y a du pour et du contre	*there are pros and cons*
les festivals sont une chose positive/négative pour un pays/une région	*festivals are positive/ negative for a country/ region*
les panneaux solaires	*solar panels*
les toilettes sèches	*dry toilets*
les véhicules électriques	*electric vehicles*
le papier recyclé	*recycled paper*

Had a look ☐ **Nearly there** ☐ **Nailed it** ☐

M
8

Extra words I should know for reading and listening activities

Le monde	The world
la pauvreté	poverty
les déchets (m)	rubbish
la surpêche	overfishing
l'empreinte carbone (f)	carbon footprint
les produits bio (m)	organic products
le covoiturage	car share
l'hébergement (m)	accommodation
l'association caritative (f)	charity organisation
les manifestations (f)	demonstrations
les pétitions (f)	petitions
les conflits (m)	conflicts
les campagnes (f)	campaigns
la sensibilisation	raising awareness
la chasse	hunting
les JO (m)	Olympic games
les habitants (m)	inhabitants
le profile	profile
les sans-abri (m)*	homeless people
l'appareil électrique (m)	electrical device
le chauffage	heating
le gobelet	tumbler
les bocaux en verre (m)	glass jars

Had a look ☐ **Nearly there** ☐ **Nailed it** ☐

Les problèmes et les solutions	Problems and solutions
se ficher de	to not care about something
réduire	to reduce
prendre conscience de	to become aware of
se plaindre	to complain
abandonner	to abandon

souligner	to underline
accueillir	to welcome
consacrer	to devote
faciliter	to facilitate
parrainer	to sponsor
inquiéter	to worry
agir	to act
mener	to lead
compter	to count
entreprendre	to undertake
lancer	to launch
tourner le dos à qqn	to turn your back on someone
donner le bras à qqn	to give someone a hand
offrir un café à qqn	to buy someone a coffee
donner un coup de poing à qqn	to hit someone
requis(e)	required
endetté(e)	indebted
festivalier	festival-goer
en tissu	made of material/cloth

Had a look ☐ **Nearly there** ☐ **Nailed it** ☐

Les expressions idiomatiques	Idioms
du coup	as a result, thus
à la fois	at the same time
en fil de fer	made of wire
en train de	in the middle of
longtemps considéré comme …	long considered as …
un milliard	a billion
des milliers**	thousands

Had a look ☐ **Nearly there** ☐ **Nailed it** ☐

M 8

★ *Sans* + noun indicates a group of people who do not possess something: homes, legal documents, etc.

Examples:

Les Sans-culottes 'The without breeches' were the common people of the lower classes in late 18th century France, lots of whom fought in the French Revolution in response to their poor quality of life.

Les sans-papiers people without papers/illegal immigrants.

 **Look for words you know already that you see within new words, for example:

mille thousand / *milliers* thousands